Light to Those in Darkness

Light to Those in Darkness

'Total Pain' and the Communion of Saints

Charlie Bell

scm press

© Charlie Bell 2023

Published in 2023 by SCM Press
Editorial office
3rd Floor, Invicta House,
108–114 Golden Lane,
London EC1Y OTG, UK

www.scmpress.co.uk

SCM Press is an imprint of Hymns Ancient & Modern Ltd
(a registered charity)

Hymns Ancient & Modern® is a registered trademark of
Hymns Ancient & Modern Ltd
13A Hellesdon Park Road, Norwich,
Norfolk NR6 5DR, UK

British Library Cataloguing in Publication data

A catalogue record for this book is available
from the British Library

978-0-334-06400-8

Typeset by Regent Typesetting
Printed and bound in Great Britain by
CPI Group (UK) Ltd

To my Piotr
and in memoriam,
Anna Matthews and Tom Hawkes

Contents

Acknowledgements

This book came out of the work that I did at St Augustine's College of Theology during my training for the sacred ministry, and so I firstly want to thank the community, the staff, the tutors and the fantastic Alan Gregory, who supervised my dissertation and encouraged me to turn it into a longer piece of work. Alan is one of a kind. I remember sitting in his office, with his and Suzy's huge dog Albert overseeing proceedings, and being in awe of someone who had such a wide range of knowledge so easily pluckable out of his brain. Alan is the reason I went to St Augustine's and the reason I enjoyed studying theology so much. I will remain endlessly grateful to him. He gave me lots of insights and help with the project and anything good in it is almost certainly down to him!

The people of St John the Divine have been a joy and privilege to serve, and I have been enormously lucky to have been surrounded by a brilliant clergy team – Fr Mark, Deacon Annie, Fr Stuart, Fr Nick, Fr Seb, Fr Peter, Fr Hamish, Fr Robert SSM – and also by a brilliant team of people who keep the show on the road – Bett, Kumba, Victor, Wail, and so many others.

I am very grateful, too, to the Bishop of Southwark, Bishop Christopher Chessun, who has been the most extraordinary help and support to me and for whom I doubtless cause a plethora of difficulties right, left and centre. I am so lucky to be in this diocese and it was an honour to be ordained priest by Bishop Christopher last year.

I remain enormously grateful to a great group of friends who attempt to keep me on the straight and narrow and are endlessly generous to me when I have quadruple booked myself. There are too many to name, and at the risk of offending those I forget, I particularly want to thank Dr Emma Syea, Fr

Tomos Reed, Fr Calum Zuckert, Mother Diane Kutar, the St Augustine's gang and Dr Harrison Carter.

I want to thank my brilliant NHS colleagues, too, for bearing with me, and my patients over the years, who continue to inspire me day by day. It has been a real joy to be included in the St Christopher's Hospice out-of-hours chaplaincy team over the past year and I am hugely grateful to the Revd Dr Andrew Goodhead for giving me the opportunity. Hospice work, and ministering among the dying, remains one of my passions, and I hope to find ways to live out what I write in the years to come. It was many years ago that I had my first medical work experience – at St Peter and St James Hospice in North Chailey – and this totally changed me and the course of what I wanted to do. Dad died at Wakefield Hospice, and the care and support he and we all were given was exemplary. The hospice movement is one of a kind and we should never stop advocating for it or being thankful for the vision of Cicely Saunders and others who gave us this huge gift.

During the production of this book, two people who have had a significant impact on me in my priestly life died, within the course of a single week. The first of these was the Revd Canon Anna Matthews, my former parish priest and Director of Ordinands. Anna is almost entirely responsible for my being ordained and her priestly identity shone out of her in everything she did. She was an absolute inspiration to generations of priests – and others – in Cambridge and beyond, and her death is both tragic and deeply felt by so many. Tom was a member of the congregation at St John the Divine, Kennington; he and his husband Frank were wonderful role models in a church that too often turns a blind eye to the fruits of same-sex relationships. Tom cared for his husband as he became unwell in later life – Frank died on the day of my first Mass, and only a few months later Tom himself died. Piotr and I were extremely fond of him and it was an honour and a privilege to bring him the Holy Communion in his last few days. If the church had more people like Anna and Tom, it would become more like the church it is called to be. May they both rest in the peace of the Lord and rise in the glory of the resurrection.

David Shervington and the team at SCM Press have been brilliant, putting up with me, making my writing so much clearer and easier to read, and giving me the chance to offer this small contribution to the field. I am enormously grateful to them. I am grateful, too, to Fr Jamie Hawley, who introduced me to the Hiroshima Report, which has proven such a fruitful conversation partner in this book.

My family, of course, have continued to tolerate my endless new ideas and inability to be in one place for any significant period of time. Losing Dad over ten years ago now made me start thinking about death and dying in a new way, and we have all grown and learnt over those years. I am so hugely lucky to have them all in my life – old and new members, young and old, living and departed. Thank you all, for everything. As this book proclaims, death is not the end, and I truly believe that those we miss remain fully a part of the communion that sustains us by their prayers. I am enormously grateful, too, to Piotr's family for making me feel so welcome, and in particular to Sylwia, Julia, the babcie and dziadkowie.

And Piotr, my Piotr. We got engaged during the production of this book, and I have never been surer, when answering a question, in my life. Piotr, you complete me – I am the luckiest person alive. Kocham Cię, babbington.

Part 1

I

Introduction

The dying have much to teach us.

Death remains, to a large degree, a taboo subject in much of the West. Despite huge mortality figures during the Covid-19 pandemic and the associated discussions of 'acceptable mortality', do-not-attempt-resuscitation orders, intensive care units and a whole host of other medical paraphernalia, the medical debate far too often remained in the abstract. Conversations in the media and elsewhere frequently focused on 'other people', or on groups of people – the 'elderly', the 'clinically extremely vulnerable', and it was far too infrequent that these groups themselves had much say in the public sphere. The reality of death was hiding in plain sight, yet very few seemed to want to go anywhere near it.

The churches, too, appeared to have little to say about death and dying. Much was made of legislation and the associated rules on social distancing, ventilation, masks, handwashing, and on those things found far more frequently within our church contexts, like the common cup for communion. But at the heart of it all was a void that never seemed to be filled – a public conversation about death itself. The churches did not appear to see the need to get such a conversation started – to bring death into the public square.

That's not to suggest that there was nothing happening on the ground. Day after day, chaplains, lay and ordained, continued their work with the sick and dying, despite restrictions imposed on them in the name of public safety. It is not the purpose of this book to attempt even a cursory review of whether the balance struck was the right one, but one thing that is objectively true is that the dying were not placed front and centre of the national pandemic response. It is now well known that many died alone, with occasional electronic communications with their loved ones at very best, and that their funeral rites, too, were curtailed. In the midst of death, we deprioritized death.

It is of course understandable that keeping people alive became a huge priority for public health leaders. What is perhaps a little less understandable is how, when a global pandemic hit, as a church we seemed to have so little to say about one of the great facts of life. I write as a priest in the Church of England, in which many, whether regular churchgoers or not, continue to be baptized, married and buried. As the established church, we surely have a responsibility to have significant ways of responding to death and dying, given our theological diversity. Yet I also write as a doctor. During my time on the oncology wards a few years ago, whenever a patient said 'Church of England', the nursing team assumed this meant they had no interest in seeing a chaplain. Have we really got to the stage where we have so little to say to the wider population about sickness, dying and death that even our chaplaincy is unwanted?

Many clergy will say that the most interesting and rewarding part of their ministry is not weddings, but funerals. There is an implicit understanding among many of us that we are often called to be with those who are in sorrow, just as much as those in joy, if not more so. Yet perhaps what is missing is an intentional focus on not only ministry but mission to those in death's grip. For many in our churches, the last rites remain an important part of life's journey, although my experience in hospital medicine would suggest that this ministry at the point of death has – to a large extent – fallen out of the wider public consciousness. Yet we are called not simply to a ministry of our own congregations, as important as that is, but to a wider ministry to those who might seek it at any stage of life.

Much has been written and debated about mission and ministry in the Church of England – and more widely – in recent years, and the falseness of the dichotomy between them is clear to see. Perhaps one of the most helpful formulations of mission and ministry that we can make use of is the Five Marks of Mission, which 'express the Anglican Communion's common commitment to, and understanding of, God's holistic and integral mission'.[1] Here, we see ministry front and centre in the life of a church of mission – where proclaiming the good news, teaching, baptizing and nurturing new believers is held alongside responding to human need by loving service and a commitment to transforming the unjust structures of society. There is no mission without ministry in a holistic and coherent church, and vice-versa, whatever the emphasis might be in any particular situation.

When we think about any of our pastoral work, it is absolutely vital that we have the ability to talk about mission as well as do it. Ministry without a missional imperative is not bad in itself, but is surely little more than what many secular organizations do, sometimes far more competently than the church itself. That's not to say that we should spend our time barracking others and demanding that proselytizing forms part of a strings-attached model of ministry – that is preparing the road to an abusive theology, and one that is unlikely to yield much good. We must, however, be able to make coherent and clear links between our mission and our ministry, our doctrine and our practice. Not to do so is both to let down the people we are called to serve, and ultimately to lose track of who and what we are as a church.

It appears that there is at the very least a missional imperative to better engagement with questions of death and dying. There is most certainly a human need (to quote the Five Marks), and because we proclaim a faith that speaks to all, there must be good news to proclaim as well. There is perhaps also a call to see the intentional addressing of the gospel to the dying as being part of the transformation of unjust structures of society. So long as we keep the dying hidden away, albeit often in plain sight, we ultimately (albeit subconsciously) dehumanize them and blot out their full dignity in order to save our embarrassment, awkwardness or discomfort. In so doing we end up doing violence to our own selves when the time comes, and we also end up embracing a less coherent, less holistic and less serious theological vision than we might otherwise have done.

While coherent theological visions might sound a little like a pipe dream, nonetheless it is essential that we commit ourselves

ιe that speaks about the world as we find it, rather
ιe wish it were. Our theology must surely include some
ιesponse to the things we don't like about life, just as
muᴄ... ᴄ the things we do. If our doctrine no longer engages
with the people and the world that we are called to serve, or
if our articulation of it is no longer intelligible or inherently
believable, then we end up preaching empty slogans, at best
shuffling off into irrelevance and at worst becoming a harmful
presence for individuals and communities alike. If our doctrine
and practice have nothing to say to the dying, then it is ques-
tionable as to whether they have anything to say to any of us.

It is for this reason that I have written this book. It is by no
means an attempt to have anything like the final word, or even
to interrogate the rich diversity of perspectives that Christian
doctrines of different hues have on death and dying. Indeed,
by focusing on just one theological motif, the communion of
saints, it is necessarily incomplete and does not address anything
like the totality of human experience or doctrinal conversation.
Similarly, the book cannot address every conception of the
human experience in focusing solely on the one key concept of
'total pain'. Yet what it does attempt to do is to call us to hold
our doctrines up to the light of human experience and learning
and ask whether we are engaging with them in ways that most
effectively speak to the world as it is. It is not ultimately asking
whether our doctrine is fit for purpose – although, of course,
that is part of the journey – but is instead asking whether the
encountering of our doctrine with the lived experience of the
people of God is reaching hearts and minds in as effective a
way as it might. It is ultimately a book about the articulation
of doctrine.

The role of doctrine in our common life

Doctrine remains something that raises hackles in the secular
world, which comes with its very own hermeneutic of suspi-
cion. Yet doctrine at its best attempts to seek the mind of God
in trying to understand, engage with and enrich human life by

focusing it all on the life that God has given us. It is proposi-
tional – it makes claims about who and what we are, who and
what God is – yet it is also relational and discursive with human
life. These things are not in opposition to one another, or at
least should not be, although there will of course be tensions
in how we develop our doctrines and how we reach truth.
Doctrine inevitably requires discernment – and it is ultimately
that discernment, and its rules of engagement, that lead to such
theological controversy.

While we will argue from a classic model of Anglican discernment in these pages,[2] it is worth stating from the outset
that the great majority of models would still require us to do
the hard work when it comes to death and dying. There are few
forms of discernment of doctrine that rely entirely on funda-
mentalist readings of scripture, and with death and dying there
is no ready-made doctrine that can be described as 'the biblical
view' without some disagreement. In fact, while Christians of
most denominations would agree that death is not the end (as
made clear in 1 Corinthians 15, among other biblical texts), it
is in many places where such agreement ends.[3] The existence
of Death, Judgement, Heaven and Hell – the Four Last Things
– is not generally disputed, but their meaning most certainly
is. There is no consensus on this even within the Church of
England, let alone more widely, and this adds to the complexity
of trying to make some sense of our doctrine in this area.

The 'Pastoral Introduction' to the *Common Worship* Funeral
Service exhibits this challenge in its vagueness:

> God's love and power extend over all creation. Every life,
> including our own, is precious to God. Christians have always
> believed that there is hope in death as in life, and that there is
> new life in Christ after death.
>
> Even those who share such faith find that there is a real
> sense of loss at the death of a loved one. We will each have
> had our own experiences of their life and death, with different
> memories and different feelings of love, grief and respect. To
> acknowledge this at the beginning of the service should help
> us to use this occasion to express our faith and our feelings

as we say farewell, to acknowledge our loss and our sorrow, and to reflect on our own mortality. Those who mourn need support and consolation. Our presence here today is part of that continuing support.[4]

What these words are actually saying about death and dying is not entirely clear, and this might be an indication that this project is futile from the start. If we cannot describe a clear theological vision about something that we will all go through, then serious questions might be raised about our purpose – our existence, even, as a body that seeks to talk about God and God's love for humankind and all creation. Fundamental to the Christian faith is faith in the life, death and resurrection of Jesus Christ, fully human and fully divine, incarnate in history and living today. Christianity appears to have both a huge amount to say about death yet, at the same time, finds it hard to say this beyond vague generalities or poetic allusions.

The same also appears true of the Easter Anthems, traditionally sung during the Easter season and taken from St Paul's letters to the Corinthians and Romans to directly address questions of death and resurrection:

Christ our passover has been sacrificed for us:
so let us celebrate the feast,
not with the old leaven of corruption and wickedness:
but with the unleavened bread of sincerity and truth.
Christ once raised from the dead dies no more:
death has no more dominion over Him.
In dying he died to sin once for all:
in living he lives to God.
See yourselves therefore as dead to sin:
and alive to God in Jesus Christ our Lord.
Christ has been raised from the dead:
the first fruits of those who sleep.
For as by man came death:
by man has come also the resurrection of the dead;
for as in Adam all die:
even so in Christ shall all be made alive.[5]

That is not to say that there are no claims made by these words, but that the tenor and the form is not necessarily one to which the contemporary world is receptive. Of course, this is not only true about death and dying – it is also true of resurrection accounts, of the form and nature of angels, and the 'already but not yet' of kingdom theology, as a few other areas where poetic truth might trump what might be described as scientific truth in producing a 'more true' account. To create a strong and implacable binary between the poetic truth and the scientific truth is a mark of current debate, but it is not how Christians have always debated and argued. It may be that one of the ways for the church to be prophetic in the twenty-first century is to find a way to speak out unapologetically in terms that refuse to be bound within that particular dialectic.

The ultimate truth proclaimed in the Anthems is found in the final line: 'even so in Christ shall all be made alive'. If 'death has no more dominion over him', it similarly has no more dominion over us, and yet we know that death still happens, and herein lies one of the great tensions of the Christian faith. We proclaim the victory of Christ over death, and yet as the *Common Worship* Preface states, 'even those who share such faith find that there is a real sense of loss at the death of a loved one'. While the careful use of language, 'a real sense of loss', does suggest that this loss may not be 'actual' in nature, nonetheless the tension shines through. How do we reconcile this grief and sense of loss with a belief in the resurrection, in the all being made alive through Christ?

Pastoral ministry and funerals

The question of reconciling grief and loss with belief in the resurrection has been present through Christian history from its earliest days, and has been engaged with and led to pastoral practice that has, at times, been radically different in nature. A good example is a comparison of the funeral services found in *Common Worship* (produced at the turn of the century for pastoral provision in the Church of England) and the Book of

Common Prayer. The tone and form (and thus ultimately the underlying belief, given the sense of *lex orandi, lex credendi*) of the two services is starkly different, and yet both remain part of the current provision of the Church of England. Neither deny either of the contrasting emotions that might be felt at the death of a loved one, but each does have a different emphasis.

The Book of Common Prayer funeral service[6] lays out a clear expectation of future life and even a timeline of that expectation, as found in the collect:

> O merciful God, the Father of our Lord Jesus Christ, who is the resurrection and the life; in whom whosoever believeth shall live, though he die; and whosoever liveth, and believeth in him, shall not die eternally; who also hath taught us (by his holy Apostle Saint Paul) not to be sorry, as men without hope, for them that sleep in him: We meekly beseech thee, O Father, to raise us from the death of sin unto the life of righteousness; that, when we shall depart this life, we may rest in him, as our hope is this our brother doth; and that, at the general Resurrection in the last day, we may be found acceptable in thy sight, and receive that blessing, which thy well-beloved Son shall then pronounce to all that love and fear thee, saying, Come, ye blessed children of my Father, receive the kingdom prepared for you from the beginning of the world: Grant this, we beseech thee, O merciful Father, through Jesus Christ, our Mediator and Redeemer. **Amen.**

Here the focus is on 'the general Resurrection in the last day', and on the 'hope' of things to come. Found, too, is significant penitential material, and the service is short to the point of being blunt. To some extent, the Book of Common Prayer appears not to offer long and ostentatious funeral rites (in contrast to some rites within the Roman Catholic medieval church, a change also seen in other Protestant churches of the period[7]) because in forming a single prayer book for the English church, Cranmer and its later compilers saw death as part of a continuum of life, which itself was explored and explained through the theology embedded in the totality of the liturgy of the Book of Common Prayer. This is not to suggest that this was not the case for the Roman Catholic Church at that time, but rather to show a clear example of where an intentionally redesigned set of liturgies saw the rightful place of death to be – as an integral part of a wider theological narrative, unexceptional and cohesive. There are, of course, other significant reasons related to the Reformation that the Book of Common Prayer made use of in this shortened and simple service, for example 'the Reformed theology of the elect' and the 'suppressing and overturning [of] traditional beliefs and customs surrounding death',[8] but it is informative that the content of the liturgy is presented as it is.

The *Common Worship* funeral material,[9] like much else in *Common Worship*, makes provision for a wide range of different theological perspectives and practices (and in doing so may not necessarily present such a clear and coherent theological narrative at first glance as the Book of Common Prayer does). It makes clear that the funeral's purpose is severalfold:

> to remember before God our *brother/sister N*;
> to give thanks for *his/her* life;
> to commend *him/her* to God our merciful redeemer and judge;
> to commit *his/her* body to be *buried/cremated*,
> and to comfort one another in our grief.

The service is longer and contains an explicit Farewell in a way that the Book of Common Prayer does not, likely reflecting both modern sensibilities and the increased number of funerals taking place for people and families for whom the day-to-day worship of the Church of England is no longer second nature. However, a key difference is the flexibility it offers, which is in direct contrast to the Book of Common Prayer, and while this does not mean that the core textual content is different, nonetheless the way the service (and thus its underlying theology) is experienced by mourners can end up fundamentally changed from that found in the core texts. Ritual – including Christian ritual – can end up changing cultural norms and expectations, and in doing so can ultimately alter public received, implicit theology.[10]

While it is not stated as one of the key aims in the Introduction, nonetheless much recent practice has seen a significant
shift away from a focus on grief towards a focus on 'celebration
of life' – a 'backward-looking' funeral that is 'judged, not by its
assurance of heavenly glory, but by whether or not it captures
the essence of the life of the departed'.[11] This is much in keeping with secular practice – as described at the start, the dying
and death remain generally taboo topics of conversation in
wider society, and thus it is a natural direction of travel to try
to remove them, as much as is practicable, from funerals themselves. This might also include funerals without the presence of
the corpse, the use of white rather than purple liturgical vestments, and the focus on tributes rather than explicitly religious
homilies that bring both the life of the deceased and the theology
of the church into conversation. Of course, this is not always
the case, but it does suggest a particular cultural trend that has
also found its way into the culture of the church.

The forms of pastoral practice at a funeral are likely to play a
significant part in the wider public understanding of the church's
perspective on death. To this end, if these 'backward-looking
funerals' become the norm, then there is a fundamental shift in
what the church appears to be saying about death and dying.
If there is little to talk about beyond death – or if what there
is to say is not readily received – then once again the dying
become a matter of embarrassment, better hidden away and
thus increasing the isolation that people who are dying might
find themselves in. Both individual and public pastoral practice,
therefore, clearly matter.

The power of liturgy to tell stories should also not be under-
estimated, and it is for this reason that the various forms of
pastoral practice, both individual and public, liturgical and
casual, are considered in Part 2 of this book. While it appeared
that there was little to be said or done in the wake of the
Covid-19 pandemic high mortality, there was a fundamentally
different situation following the death of Queen Elizabeth II. It
is noticeable that there has been very limited traction in terms
of memorial events or corporate liturgies for those who have
died from Covid-19, whereas the death of the monarch created

not only a huge outpouring of grief but also the need for this grief to be somehow held – curated, even – by some entity in public life. The church, and the Church of England in particular, was the most visible agent of this, and it became clear that, for regular worshippers and for those with little to no interest or engagement with the church, nonetheless the televised funeral service for the Queen played a pivotal role in providing a space for that grief to be held, and just as importantly for some of the rawness of that grief to be laid down.

Despite much said to the contrary over the preceding years, it was clear that in the midst of a period of national mourning, the Church of England retained a particular place in the corporate life of the nation. It is noticeable, too, that the funeral itself was not a 'celebration of life' but rather a traditional, forward-looking laying to rest of an elderly monarch, whose life had much to celebrate within it and yet whose death triggered significant feelings of loss and genuine sadness. To date, it is not clear that the church has built on this experience in anything like the positive way it might and, as during the Covid-19 pandemic, there was very limited theological narrative about death itself beyond the confines of the liturgy (a liturgy that was both sacred and secular, and yet which gathered itself around the reality of death in both forms). There is an urgent need for the church to do so not only from a missional but from a ministerial perspective – once again, these two finding themselves to be two sides of the same coin, most particularly when speaking to and ministering among those 'in darkness and in the valley of the shadow of death'.

The gift of doctrine to pastoral practice

We can see, therefore, that there are tensions in what Christians believe (or do not believe) in the expression of these beliefs, in the inherent challenge of expressing and holding beliefs in the life beyond without losing sight of the very real human feelings of grief and loss at the death of a loved one, and often at contemplation of one's own mortality and death. There are tensions, too, in the pastoral practice that, at best, embodies these beliefs and makes them more widely known. So what might an enunciation of these beliefs look like? Or rather, how might we find a way to enunciate something that remains intangible and yet we believe to be true – that death is not the end?

It is worth, at this point, summarizing some of our thinking up until now. As a church, we need to find a way to describe, believe, proclaim and embody in each part of our corporate life that, through his resurrection, Jesus Christ has defeated death once and for all, and in so doing has given us a sure hope that our own death will not be the end of our life with him. We need to find a way to do this that recognizes the contingency of our language and the incompleteness of anything we might try to say on the matter. We need to find a way to do it, too, that is steeped in the history and traditions of the church, and that finds its seed and direction in the pages of scripture. We need, in other words, to find ways to make use of our doctrine that will enable us to speak more clearly about the Christian hope beyond death, and to do so in a way that does not prevent further exploration and imagination. Fundamentally, too, we need to ensure that any doctrine we proclaim is held in conversation with the reality of human experience, not necessarily to redefine or change it, but to refine it and interrogate it, to bring it closer to a true definition of the reality it is attempting to describe. That, we must recognize, is the role of theology.

It is here that the words of 1 Corinthians 15.51 become so helpful to any discussion, pastoral or academic, of the reality of death: 'Listen, I will tell you a mystery!' The language of mystery can be overused, but appears to be an entirely appropriate word to discuss an attempt to elucidate and discuss things that are beyond human understanding and the competence of human speech, which fit into the category of 'I know this', even if I don't know the fullness of what 'this' is. In being comfortable in speaking of mystery, we immediately lose the desperate human need to produce simple classifications, and are able to hold even contradictions more easily because we know our theology reaches for something beyond what we can ever truly define. Our doctrine intentionally becomes a work in progress rather than the finished article.

An immediate challenge to this might be the difficulty that it could present to our ability to engage with the wider world. It is beyond the scope of this book to fully engage with that question, but it is by no means clear that this is the inevitable outcome. In recent years, the Church of England has on occasion appeared curiously unwilling to speak in imaginative terms, preferring instead to use 'accessible' terms that run the risk of losing sight of the mysterious at the heart of the Christian faith. While it is commendable to present the faith in understandable terms, nonetheless it is important not to lose track of the fundamental absolute unknowability of much of the Christian worldview, not as something incidental but as central to the proclaimed and accepted ultimate human unknowability of the mind of God. It is the premise of this book that the more who challenge the development and interrogation of our doctrines the more likely it is to lead to a healthier and more coherent Christianity.

By doing this, doctrine becomes not the untouchable shibboleth that binds our theology in chains, but rather takes its rightful place as a living tradition, grounded in the theological virtues of faith, hope and love, which can continually give new insights into the questions, concerns, beliefs, hopes and fears of each generation. Our doctrines, if they are true, cannot be threatened by being challenged or engaged with in new ways, with the new information that we find through human discovery. Our doctrines, instead, must surely prove most useful when they are in dialogue with human experience and through such dialogue inform our response to such experience. In doing so, they strengthen and improve our pastoral practice, enabling us to do as we proclaim.

Total pain and the communion of saints

This book, then, undertakes precisely that kind of theological enterprise – considering the concept of 'total pain' (as described by Dame Cicely Saunders of the hospice movement) in the light of the doctrine of the communion of saints. 'Total pain', as a concept, already has theological underpinnings and has done so since its formulation. The purpose of this book is to hold up the questions raised by this idea in the light of the doctrine of the communion of saints and enable a conversation between the two. It interrogates the theology behind and the implications of a belief in the doctrine of the communion of saints, and asks what such a lived doctrine might offer to developing a theological response to 'total pain'. It seeks to develop a Christian anthropology that is better able to serve those in despair and shed light on the role of the communion in this endeavour, and it looks to the pastoral out-flowing of this kind of anthropology as shaped by both doctrine and experience, and by the interaction between the two.

It does so with a view to both the ministry and mission of the church. In refusing to turn away from questions of good news for those in 'total pain', it seeks to embed ministerial provision in a theological exploration of the consequences of a particular Christian doctrine. It looks for ways to properly address and get alongside those experiencing existential dread and refuses to acknowledge that they are outside the love and purview of Christ, while concurrently refusing to ignore their experience. It seeks to affirm faith, hope and love, while refusing to ignore the reality of pain, suffering, sadness and grief.

The dying have much to teach us. So far, much of what we have said seems to point the other way – that we must find ways to talk to the dying. In some ways, this is the challenge – the church has not found its voice to communicate the good news to the dying effectively in contemporary society. Yet such communication can never be one way, and if we fall into that trap then we undo much of the good work we could otherwise do. In finding ways to talk to the dying, we must find ways to dwell among them, too. In doing both of those things, we find ways not only to refine our self-understanding as Christian community but to find better ways to talk about the Christian life in its entirety too. Discussions about death are never separate from conversations about life, if we approach them from a Christian standpoint – they are two ways of looking at life in communion, here on earth and beyond the grave. Before we turn to that fellowship and communion in Christ, let us first consider a key and enduring part of human life which we often would rather pretend did not exist – pain.

Notes

1 Anglican Communion, 'Marks of Mission', www.anglicancom munion.org/mission/marks-of-mission.aspx (accessed 30.11.2022).

2 Readers may like to consult Mark Chapman, Sathianathan Clarke and Martyn Percy, eds, *The Oxford Handbook of Anglican Studies* (Oxford: Oxford University Press, 2015), most particularly Chapter 9.

3 Readers may like to consult Bart D. Ehrman, *Heaven and Hell: A History of the Afterlife* (New York: Simon and Schuster, 2020).

4 Church of England, 'Funeral', www.churchofengland.org/prayer-and-worship/worship-texts-and-resources/common-worship/death-and-dying/funeral#mm121 (accessed 15.11.2022).

5 Church of England, 'The Easter Anthems', www.churchofengland.org/prayer-and-worship/worship-texts-and-resources/common-worship/common-material/canticles-main-12 (accessed 12.6.2022).

6 Church of England, 'At the Burial of the Dead', www.church ofengland.org/prayer-and-worship/worship-texts-and-resources/book-common-prayer/burial-dead (accessed 2.12.2022).

7 Readers may like to consult Philip Booth and Elizabeth Tingle, eds, *A Companion to Death, Burial, and Remembrance in Late Medieval and Early Modern Europe, c. 1300–1700* (Leiden: Brill, 2020).

8 Paul Thomas, *Using the Book of Common Prayer* (London: Church House Publishing, 2012), p. 23.

9 Church of England, Funeral, www.churchofengland.org/prayer-and-worship/worship-texts-and-resources/common-worship/death-and-dying/funeral#mm121 (accessed 15.11.2022).

10 Bernard Cooke and Gary Macy, *Christian Symbol and Ritual: An Introduction* (Oxford: Oxford University Press, 2005), pp. 161–71.

11 John Lampard, 'The Future of Christian Funerals in the Methodist Church', *The Epworth Review*, www.methodist.org.uk/our-faith/life-and-faith/theology/the-epworth-review/ (accessed 2.12.2022).

2

Pain – an exploration

What is evil, and why does God permit it?

This must be one of the most perennial questions of humanity, pervading different religious, cultural, contextual, philosophical, political and societal traditions, thought-systems and viewpoints. The mere existence of evil has led some to question the nature and love of God, as Hume's well-known rhetoric (following Epicurus) suggests: 'Is God willing to prevent evil, but not able? Then he is not omnipotent. Is he able, but not willing? Then he is malevolent. Is he both able and willing? Then from whence comes evil?'[1] There is, thus, an inherent tension in the Christian religion, in which God's goodness and sole creativity appear to contradict the possibility of evil's existence. It is possible to respond to such questioning through refutation, defence or theodicy, although the history of Christian theology suggests that none is entirely competent in producing a comprehensive response.[2] That the origin and existence of evil is a mystery, rather than a problem, might appear the most appropriate description[3] – an experience of human life that cannot be fully explained and whose ultimate aetiology cannot be determined.

Much has been written about the nature and origin of evil, and it is well beyond the scope of this book to consider the totality of it here. However, a key insight from Christian literature on this topic is to recognize the mysterious nature of evil, and in so doing to avoid attempting a neatly packaged theodicy, and instead to begin our thinking by addressing evil from a phenomenological perspective: evil exists, however we might define that term. We see evil in the world, and we recognize – often in a universally human way – when things are not as we innately believe they should be. Whether this is the death of a child, or poverty and hunger, or death by sudden natural disaster, we can point to certain things in the world and feel the need to ask why. These are not petty injustices – they are significant and serious challenges to our conception of the good.

Sometimes these examples of evil appear to come from the 'natural world'. One argument posited is that there is an inevitability to these things we interpret as evil, and not merely from the well-rehearsed 'free will' argument.[4] They are a result, perhaps, of evolutionary processes; they are necessary to enable life to flourish. We might think in this case of the tendency towards violence and competition in theories of evolution, and ask how this is compatible with the idea of a loving and good creator God.[5] Science offers us certain explanations of the natural world which may sit uncomfortably with what our faith holds to be true. Beyond the literalist arguments from Genesis and seven-day creation, evolution does present a challenge to the Christian narrative that all God created was 'good'.

We might think here of viruses or cancer. How might we call these things ontologically 'good'? Much has been written about these very questions,[6] primarily focusing on the necessity of certain processes for viable life to continue, and yet this does not take away from the immediate – if necessary – evil that is felt even in service of the 'greater good'. Evil experienced may not be the same as evil extant (similar, perhaps, to the 'loss felt' not necessarily reflecting actual loss, as discussed in the Introduction), and yet nonetheless the human experience cannot be shut out by a vague and abstract reference to this 'greater good'. If each person is truly created in the image of God, then Christian theology cannot afford to ignore the actual experience of individual people, even if it might seek to situate this experience in a wider theological narrative.

It may be that one of the key responsibilities of a Christian theology that rightly takes note of that *imago Dei* is to hold the reality of human experience in the same theological cauldron as our overarching doctrine, of a good God who loves each of God's children infinitely and without exception. These two things may seem at tension. They may helpfully challenge the theologian to avoid easy answers and aid them to avoid any attempt to claim knowledge and understanding that is rightly God's. Yet for the individual this tension may feel less creative and more painful. There is a need for pastoral sensitivity in any expression of doctrine, but in cases like this it becomes particularly acute. The theologian cannot be separate from the world as it is, or from the lives of the people of God as they experience them.

As I have written elsewhere, in some cases it seems appropriate that human experience – together with scientific enquiry – might make us refine our doctrine and lead to potentially surprising outcomes. In matters of human sexuality, for example, it appears to me that the challenge of experience and discovery to doctrine might lead to a refinement of that doctrine, a refinement through careful interrogation in the light of scripture.[7] However, in some cases, a process of continual refinement nonetheless leads us to what remains irreconcilable. This looks to be the case in the reflection on evil; it is surely a cheapened, and not an enriched, form of theology that doesn't raise at least some voice of protest at the death of children. As we shall see, this theology has a rich biblical history (including, for example, certain psalms and even, in some readings, the weeping of Christ for his friend Lazarus), and yet it remains challenging to the Christian mindset to remain angry at God. All that said, the story of Job does not dismiss that anger and sense of injustice out of hand; it does, however, appear to 'eschew explanation for yet other ways of rendering enigmas intelligible'.[8] Herein lies the tension in our ongoing theological journey with God.

We have briefly considered the appeal to the natural world as at least a partial explanation for the existence of some forms of evil. This is clearly not the only possible explanation for evils suffered, and we cannot extricate human agency from much that we might call evil, either in the cause of such evil or in the response to it. Historically, there have been several different forms of evil described, which themselves may require different responses, both theologically and practically. Swinburne describes moral evil as 'including all bad states caused deliberately by humans doing what they believe to be bad, and especially wrong (or allowed to occur by humans negligently failing to do what they believe to be good)' (with echoes of the General Confession of the Book of Common Prayer) and 'also the bad states constituted by such deliberate actions or negligent failure'.[9] Natural evil, conversely, 'includes all the trail of suffering which disease and accidents unpreventable by man bring in their train',[10] which might include natural disasters and disease.

Of course, it is not at all clear that these two forms of evil are entirely separate. While the link between 'moral evil' and the existence of sin is clear, Swinburne suggests a link with natural evil too, as it 'includes the bad desires with which we find ourselves: the temptations to take more than our fair share of the world's goods, to lie and deceive for the sake of our reputation'.[11] Thus, the outcome or state of natural evil has complicated aetiology – while some natural disasters are entirely without human cause, some are entirely related to human agency (for example climate change, exploitative farming practices) and some deliver extremely poor states of being because of the response of human beings to such natural events (for example starvation in parts of sub-Saharan Africa following natural drought).

In addition, both forms of evil suffered may be ameliorated, at least in part, by the goodness of others in responding to the evil. A frequent preachers' refrain, for example, heard in response to questions of 'Where was God in the tsunami?' has been, 'In the people looking after the injured and dead, providing food for the hungry,' and so on. To recognize this in the context of questions of evil, however, is to say that doing so is more significant than being a 'good person', or – more theologically – a 'good neighbour'. Much more than this, it is suggesting that by being that good neighbour, we end up participating in the response of God to evil – we take on a role that is itself intensely theological. We say something, therefore, about the necessity of Christian solidarity in the face of evil, not as an optional yet life-giving extra but as a fundamental element of the Christian worldview not only of citizenship of the Kingdom but of our basic anthropology. To respond in solidarity (either as agents of the mercy of God, or responding in a 'humane' or more fully human way in terms of sociality, as we shall see) is to actively participate in God's response to evil, and to participate is to realize our humanity more fully.

Beyond the individual

The particular form of evil examined in our argument here is pain. In considering pain, we will see that the clear and easy line of separation between moral and natural evil is little more than an illusion. We must seek a more helpful response to the existential questions that are raised by the incomprehensibility of the circumstances we find ourselves in despite our belief in the goodness of God and God's love for us. One way of doing this might be to reconceptualize our understanding of evil itself, focus less on trying to nail down the particularities of its aetiology on each occasion, and instead recognize that both cause and effect require a human response, which is a better focus than frustration at God's unwillingness to act to restore justice.

In doing so, we move beyond a need to allocate blame – blame of God for God's perceived poverty of insight in creation, blame of God for not intervening, blame of others for their perpetration of 'moral evils', blame of ourselves for not avoiding such evil, blame of others for not caring enough in the aftermath, and so on. Instead, perhaps, we might reframe the problem of evil within the context of Christian solidarity, a solidarity that is ultimately bound up with and explained by the theological motif of communion. We will return to this in greater detail in Part 2, but for now it is helpful for us to recognize that this requires a shift from understanding the Christian experience in purely individual terms – an individual as separate from a wider body, albeit living among others – towards an understanding of an individual-in-communion.

This is not the same as blurring the existence of the individual into an amorphous communitarian entity in which one's own experience is subjugated, subverted or ultimately ignored in the service of the wider group. To do so would be to ignore the *imago Dei* and hence to move beyond the bounds of Christian thought and historical theological exploration. It is, however, to recognize the ultimate interconnectedness of human life (and, perhaps, beyond this to the whole of creation), and – as we shall see – in a way that goes beyond death and includes the saints living and departed. In Chapter 6, we shall consider the implications of such a doctrine, and may find ourselves challenged by how we might set boundaries around the inclusion within (or exclusion from) such a communion. For the time being we need focus only on the radical claims such a doctrine might make on our understanding of evil and, specifically, pain.

If we follow this line of thinking, whereby our experiences must be held within the solidarity of communion, then pain, while experienced most intensely by the individual, is not *solely* an individual experience. We must be careful here not to negate the importance of pain for the individual in our search for solidarity, but our theological reflections here are not dissimilar to explorations in anthropology and sociology that understand pain, at least in part, as a social phenomenon. This suggests that we might expect the wider body of people to have an impact on the body of the individual experiencing pain, in terms of its conception intellectually, as well as its emotional tolerability, its form of expression and its acceptability societally. It is this complex conversation, to-and-fro between individual sufferer and community, to which our doctrine of the communion of saints must be able to speak.

This is in many ways easier to speak of in abstract terms by the theologian than it is for the immediate sufferer of pain, and, as we have said, there is a serious need for pastoral sensitivity for any engagement in this area. Yet we shall also see that failure to develop the theology in the first place for fear of pastoral insensitivity does no favours either to the sufferer (most particularly the future sufferer) or to the wider body of Christ, about whom this problem speaks, far beyond the immediate context of pain suffered by an individual. This search for and grasping towards self-understanding is one of the key purposes of theology, and at its best theology can hold up a mirror to some of our cultural and contextual preconceptions and demand we address the flaws it identifies.

Before we focus again on the different meanings of pain, it is worth giving an example in this area, to begin our exploration of the complexity that underlies any discussion of a socio-psycho-biological process such as pain. We have previously spoken about the lack of precision in the division between moral and natural evil. Let us take the example of the person who is found to have caused grievous bodily harm to a stranger in the street. A common response would be to blame the 'aggressor', to assert that they are responsible for their actions and, because of this, should be punished. This is certainly the current overriding cultural expectation in the UK – we may consider extenuating circumstances over and above this, but these are the exception. This is seen in social norms institutionalized by and in law.

Putting aside the possibility that the person might have been directly provoked (and the complicated moral implications of this), let us imagine that this person did undertake a moment of significant and random violence in the street. In the morning of this day, that same person was beaten by his employer, an occurrence he faces on a daily basis. Do we therefore change our opinion on blame? He also lives in poverty, because of a reliance on alcohol and illicit drugs. He turned to the use of drugs because of an abusive childhood. In addition, he has a genetic susceptibility to addiction, and has learned behaviours from violence in childhood.

All this is to say that in this situation, the complexity of the underlying dynamics might not remove the need for justice or a recognition of individual responsibility, but nonetheless a quick and often simplistic reasoning that moves us unthinkingly between correlation and causation, and towards culpability and blame, needs to be challenged from a variety of different perspectives. As we look towards the various causes and conceptions of pain, we will meet many of the biological processes that we find involved in most, if not all, human experiences. We may find that the complexity of relationship between the different contributory factors in the biological and social reality of human existence is, in fact, better explained by the idea of communion than by more individualistic or communitarian understandings of the human person.

Our understanding of life as communion must also, surely, lead us to finding better ways to allocate blame (if that is the right way to think about it), and better ways to engage with fellow Christians − and others − when they face existential dread and the potential associated despair. A recognition of the complexity of human life and our connectedness to one another must, too, make us reconsider responsibility, both our obligations to one another in our response to social phenomena such as pain, and our recognition of the role we − individually and corporately − may have played in others' despair. Interconnectedness of human existence, in its various forms, has significant implications.

The meaning of pain

Let us turn, now, to a focus on pain itself. The first question we might ask ourselves is whether categorizing it as an evil is entirely justified. We have considered the evolutionary argument above − that some processes are necessary in order to allow a greater good − and pain sits squarely within this kind of thinking. Pain at its simplest can be argued to be the body's best defence against further damage, the classic example being the reflex loop that ensures we withdraw our hand upon touching a hot surface. The implications of such a pain system being absent are obvious and can be seen in the loss of feeling and subsequent damage done to the toes of those who suffer from uncontrolled diabetes. In this case, the benefits of pain are entirely absent: with a raised blood glucose the nerves become damaged over time, preventing any signals of damage reaching the brain and damage being done to the soft tissue of the foot. The short-term benefit of no pain quickly leads to long-term problems. Pain is not the enemy here.

Yet pain does not always appear to be proportionate to the damage it seeks to avoid. For those suffering from chronic pain

– particularly primary chronic pain, in which 'no underlying condition adequately accounts for the pain or its impact'[12] – the potential benefits of such pain ensuring the avoidance of damage appear to be fairly clearly outweighed by the ongoing disability that such pain creates. Such disability is likely not only to be physical in nature but also to entail forms of mental or psychological suffering, reductions in normal social and societal functioning, and – particularly for those open to such a worldview – a level of spiritual suffering too.

In the next chapter, we shall address pain from the perspective of hospice care and meet the concept of 'total pain', which offers a more holistic understanding than a merely biological perspective might do. Here, however, we will focus on the commonly discussed 'biopsychosocial' model of pain. It is a model that is challenged by the idea of 'total pain' but nonetheless offers a framework through which to explore the 'complex interaction of biological, psychological, and social variables' that 'shape the person's perception and response to illness' rather than a more simplistic biomedical model of disease.[13] The interaction of these different factors is complex and remains an area of active research.[14]

The general view of such a model is well described as follows:

Pain is a subjective perception that results from the transduction, transmission, and modulation of sensory input filtered through a person's genetic composition, prior learning history, and modulated further by their current physiological status, idiosyncratic appraisals, expectations, current mood state, and sociocultural environment.[15]

This particular model is, however, primarily related to an individual's response to physical pain. Another key contribution to pain as an experience is emotional or psychological pain – not the psychological consequences of physical pain, but rather a pain that springs from mental distress. While medically the underlying aetiology may be different (although there are suggestions that the underlying neural mechanisms may not be entirely distinct[16]), there has been increased recognition in recent years that such pain can be as debilitating as physical pain and may also best be described in similar terms.

The causes of this mental pain are complex: they may relate to processes whose source is directly psychological, including mental illness; to what might best be seen as socio-psychological (for example, feelings of shame or embarrassment that are felt as mental pain and have their source in a social context); or are a consequence of a physical disability or illness. Each of these causes – and different underlying sources of pain – are then processed and expressed by a particular individual in a way that attempts to make sense of the underlying experience and process. It is likely that any attempt to overly systematize or try to attain absolute objectivity in matters of pain in terms of cause or causes will ultimately prove fruitful.

The definition of 'pain', therefore, cannot be easily delineated into the purely physical and the purely mental. The crossover in terms of subjective experience of these different forms of pain means that they might be better understood as part of the same phenomenon rather than as two substantially different phenomena. As we shall see in our discussion of 'total pain', Cicely Saunders was arguably quite ahead of her time in her intuition that this was the case. Before we turn to how this wider conception of pain might help us in our theological explorations of it, we must briefly consider the concept of mental illness and mental distress.

Pain in mental illness

So far, we have considered pain as part of the continuum of human experience, as something not entirely bad in and of itself (and which may contain within it an expression of meaning, as we shall see below) and yet something that can prove deeply difficult to live with. Having specifically mentioned mental pain, it is worth outlining in clear terms what this book is not attempting to do: it does not attempt a spiritualization or theologization of psychiatric morbidity.

It is important to state this point because it remains a temptation within some parts of the church to try to find ways to 'explain away' mental illness (in particular by association with Satan, for example in some branches of Pentecostalism[17]). We shall meet the church's wider discomfort with issues of despair and dereliction in the next chapter and see how its attitude can, if not carefully interrogated, lead to a deeply unhelpful outlook, both pastorally and theologically. In recent years, work has been done to address this risk from within the Christian community, and it is recognized that while we cannot (and should not) separate our faith worldview and perspective from our understanding of illness, there is nonetheless an important difference between doing so and denying scientific understandings.[18] This is a fine balance. As we have discussed, theology must surely embrace the totality of human life, but at the same time should ensure that it is answering questions proper to it rather than attempting to find answers where other disciplines might be better placed to do so.

For our purposes here, it is important to describe the hermeneutic with which mental pain is being addressed in these pages. From our perspective, we see mental illness, and mental ill health, on a similar footing to physical health – that is, as an ultimately biological set of mechanisms (albeit with complex and multilevel causes). In so doing, we argue against the stigma often felt by those with mental illness who are made to feel that their illness is somehow 'less than' physical illness or in some way 'all in the mind' and hence 'less real'. We remain open to the role of God in all things and all forms of illness – physical and mental – but in doing so do not ignore the fundamental role of the natural sciences in finding useful and empirical explanations for biological processes. We do so because to spiritualize mental (or, indeed, physical) pain is to ignore the huge gains in understanding in this area and therefore, ultimately, to harm those for whom this is a daily reality.

In our discussion of 'total pain', we will meet Saunders' conception of spiritual aspects of pain. To argue for a primarily biological understanding is not to negate this, nor is it to negate the social aspects or sociological causes of pain. Biological mechanisms are, ultimately, the final pathway through which pain is mediated (whatever the original causes or our ways of describing them), and thus any attempt to ignore the biology will prove fruitless. This is not a reductionist argument: it does not suggest that there are not different ways of conceiving of this pain, or of thinking about its ultimate causes. Similarly, it is not an argument for simply treating pain like any other biological phenomenon, not least because we know empirically that pain does not yield in such a way. Simply treating physical pain with analgesics, for example, might not work, as we see in the current NICE guidelines on chronic pain.[19] We will return to these, and similar, questions in the next chapter; for now, it is enough to make clear that our model involves synthesis between, and not incompatibility of, our different conceptions of pain. It is for this reason that we address it as a phenomenon rather than as a purely biological entity – but also for this reason that we refuse to ignore its biology too.

A clarification must also be made on the topic of mental pain. Mental – or psychological, psychogenic, emotional – pain may have a number of different causes or specific aetiologies, and one class of these will be mental illnesses. We know that chronic illness, including pain-based syndromes, is often associated with poor mental health, and this may result in diagnosable conditions such as anxiety or depression. There is evidence of bidirectionality in this relationship, and there may be shared neural mechanisms that account for this.[20] There remains debate in psychiatry as to whether we best diagnose patients using a categorical approach (which 'relies on diagnostic criteria to determine the presence or absence' of illness) or a dimensional approach (which 'places such behaviours on a continuum of frequency and/or severity'),[21] but for now it is worth stating that certain conditions, such as major depression, anxiety or schizophrenia, are diagnosed as discrete illnesses and move beyond poor mental health to describe a particular set of symptoms that, found together, describe a particular condition.

In our discussion of 'total pain', we must be alert to the risk of ignoring discrete mental illness in pursuit of a holistic understanding of pain. While some of the principles that we employ may provide us with significant insights into cause and effect, and potential treatments or pastoral engagement – whether utilizing the biopsychosocial model or Saunders' model – we must not lose sight of the potential for discrete illnesses that might better be primarily conceptualized as mental illness (rather than seeing the mental distress as a part of a pain phenomenological continuum). This requires attentiveness, but it appears clear that Saunders herself had no intention of ignoring other models of illness in her development of her own. It is also not to say that her model has nothing to say to models of mental illness; as discussed above, there remains some debate as to how best to diagnose forms of mental illness and whether our current discrete diagnoses remain entirely fit for purpose.

The relationship between these different elements may be quite complicated, yet we would surely be doing a dying person a disservice if we refused to countenance their being depressed and instead wished to conceptualize their mental state entirely in terms of existential dread or despair. These terms may prove more useful to the theologian or pastor than to the doctor, but similarly we must try not to draw too fine a distinction between the two (the author has a particular stake in this claim!). One of the great challenges of psychiatry is converting the subjective experience of patients into clinically useful criteria. Similarly, the theologian or pastor must carefully ensure that the language they use to describe the human experience is true to both the experience itself and to their underlying doctrinal and pastoral understanding.

Pain as meaning

This leads us to an important facet of pain that we must not ignore, whether as clinician, pastor or theologian: pain as meaning. In our discussion above, we spoke of existential dread and despair, which themselves are terms that situate subjective experiences of pain in their wider context. Despair – the absence of hope – may be how a patient describes the sum of their pain and may relate to their facing death or simply facing a life they no longer feel is worth living. As we have described, such a person may be suffering from diagnosable depression (with the biological and psychological features it entails), but they may instead be experiencing a pain that does not fit into this diagnosis, yet, through this interpretative lens, has a significant impact on their worldview and their ability to function. It is important to recognize that pain-as-meaning will also shake us from our own particular cultural worldview. It is for this reason that while Saunders' conception of 'total pain' may speak to us in a particular culture, place and time, her definitions and thinking may not be entirely applicable to people for whom our own cultural assumptions are not second nature. Sarah Coakley makes reference to this in her Introduction to *Pain and Its Transformations*, a volume that 'set out to probe [the] mystery' of pain, recognizing that 'the way we interpret our pain is all important for the mode of our suffering of it'.[22] This volume discusses the '*meanings* of pain that different cultures, ethnicities, and religions ascribe to pain, thereby mediating – often through meditative, musical, and ritual enactment – a narrative that transcends the individual sufferer and so gives public expression to private agony'.

Saunders' conception of 'total pain' is an attempt to draw together the different facets of pain that we have explored in this chapter, and in doing so forge an understanding that offers some kind of systematic way of exploring the meaning of the pain felt when facing death or when life is no longer felt to offer hope. Her model does not necessitate a singular meaning to pain, but nonetheless situates an exploration of meaning within an explicitly Christian theological vision. In so doing, her model does not stop at explanation but also points towards how we might take that understanding and develop it pastorally.

By exploring Saunders' vision with an intentional focus on its relationship with a particular theological motif, we aim to further explore what pastoral and 'ritual enactment' might accompany this understanding and test it as a 'narrative' that might link the individual expression to the overarching theological account that we hold as Christians. It is to the task of unpacking her vision that we now turn.

Notes

1 Michael Hickson, 'A brief history of problems of evil', in Justin McBrayer and Daniel Howard-Snyder, eds, *The Blackwell Companion to the Problem of Evil* (Hoboken: Wiley-Blackwell, 2014), pp. 6–7.

2 Michael Murray, 'Theodicy', in Thomas Flint and Michael Rea, eds, *The Oxford Handbook of Philosophical Theology* (Oxford: Oxford University Press, 2009), p. 365.

3 David Holley, *Meaning and Mystery: What It Means to Believe in God* (Oxford: Blackwell, 2010), p. 8.

4 A discussion of this topic is available in Laura W. Ekstrom, *God, Suffering, and the Value of Free Will* (Oxford: Oxford University Press, 2021).

5 William Stahl, Robert Campbell, Yvonne Petry, Gary Diver, *Webs of Reality: Social Perspectives on Science and Religion* (Piscataway: Rutgers University Press, 2002), pp. 153–6.

6 An excellent example is Leonard M. Hummel and Gayle E. Woloschak, *Chance, Necessity, Love: An Evolutionary Theory of Cancer* (Eugene: Cascade, 2017).

7 Charlie Bell, *Queer Holiness* (London: Darton, Longman & Todd, 2022).

8 David B. Burrell, *Deconstructing Theodicy: Why Job has Nothing to Say to the Puzzle of Suffering* (Grand Rapids: Brazos, 2008), p. 123.

9 Richard Swinburne, *Providence and the Problem of Evil* (Oxford: Oxford University Press, 1998), p. 145.

10 Swinburne, *Providence*, p. 150.

11 Swinburne, *Providence*, p. 152.

12 National Institute for Health and Care Excellence, 'Chronic pain (primary and secondary) in over 16s: assessment of all chronic pain and management of chronic primary pain: NICE guideline [NG193]', 7 April 2021, www.nice.org.uk/guidance/ng193/chapter/recommendations (accessed 04.01.2022).

13 Dennis C. Turk, Hilary Wilson and Kimberly S. Swanson, 'The biopsychosocial model of pain and pain management', in Michael H. Ebert and Robert D. Kerns, eds, *Behavioural and Psychopharmacologic Pain Management* (Cambridge: Cambridge University Press, 2011), p. 16.

14 An interesting introduction to current thinking is available here: Mustafa al'Absi and Magne Arve Flaten, eds, *The Neuroscience of Pain, Stress, and Emotion* (London: Elsevier, 2016).

15 Turk, Wilson and Swanson, 'The biopsychosocial model of pain and pain management', p. 16.

16 Annamarie Cano, Jaclyn Heller Issner and Courtney L. Dixon, 'Couple and family psychotherapeutic approaches to pain management',

in Michael H. Ebert and Robert D. Kerns, eds, *Behavioural and Psychopharmacologic Pain Management* (Cambridge: Cambridge University Press, 2011), p. 240.

17 See particularly Chapter 11 in Allan Anderson, *An Introduction to Pentecostalism: Global Charismatic Christianity* (Cambridge: Cambridge University Press, 2004).

18 For a discussion, see Christopher C. H. Cook and Isabelle Hamley, *The Bible and Mental Health* (London: SCM Press, 2020).

19 See the NICE guidelines referred to in note 12 above.

20 W. Michael Hooten, 'Chronic Pain and Mental Health Disorders: Shared Neural Mechanisms, Epidemiology, and Treatment', *Mayo Clinic Proceedings* 91(7) (July 2016), pp. 955–70; and Jiyao Sheng et al., 'The Link between Depression and Chronic Pain: Neural Mechanisms in the Brain', *Neural Plast.* (2017, Article 9724371)

21 Angela D. Moreland and Jean E. Dumas, 'Categorical and Dimensional Approaches to the Measurement of Disruptive Behaviour in the Preschool Years: A meta-analysis', *Clinical Psychology Review* 28(6) (July 2008), pp. 1059–1070.

22 Sarah Coakley, 'Introduction', in Sarah Coakley and Kay Kaufman Shelemay, eds, *Pain and Its Transformations: The Interface of Biology and Culture* (Cambridge: Harvard University Press, 2007), p. 1.

3

Total pain and its theological repercussions

The concept of 'total pain' was first fully described by Dame Cicely Saunders, a social worker turned physician whose life's work was fundamentally coloured by her Christian faith.[1] Saunders herself described such pain as 'including not only physical symptoms but also mental distress and social or spiritual problems'.[2] Since its introduction this concept has influenced the developing practice of palliative care – and, on occasion, other disciplines too. Saunders ultimately saw the purpose of such care as being 'space for freedom of spirit in facing the mystery of death',[3] and described her own journey towards developing the concept in narrative terms: in encounter with others, in following them as individuals with stories and histories, and as people with an integrity that included mind, body, spirit and community. The holistic, narrative understanding of the human person that Saunders utilized is the hermeneutical key, and found also at the heart of the doctrine of the communion of saints.

Saunders' concept of total pain developed over time. It was primarily a new conceptual approach that then led to her calls to rethink the treatment of such pain. She thought intentionally about the terminally ill's experience of pain, when 'there is nothing more to be done'.[4] This became 'the starting point for an emergent medicine of terminal care, central to which is a multi-facetted understanding of pain ... a medicine concerned also for the meaning of pain'.[5] She highlighted the need to 'question the pain [the patient] endures and seek meaning in it', and David Clark, one of the key experts on her life and work, suggests that this broke the biomedical mould, allowing 'the finest human sentiments to shine through'.[6] Clark quotes a well-known passage of Saunders' from the *Nursing Mirror*, in which a patient described not only her back pain but also the financial situation of her son and husband, her own emotional pain, and her ability to 'begin to feel safe again'. Saunders says of this description: 'Without any further questioning she had talked of her mental as well as physical distress, of her social problems and of her spiritual need for security,'[7] This openness to experience in its widest sense marks out much of Saunders' vision.

Her conceptualization took shape not as an attempt to facilitate a sanitized, 'clean death, death that does not disturb too much', as Stanley Hauerwas describes modern death, but rather to understand death as a part, and destination, of an individual's life journey. Hauerwas describes death as something for which to prepare: 'one where life's work is over ... moral obligations to dependants discharged ... not an outrage, or tempt[ing] others to rage or despair; and my dying is not marred by unbearable, degrading pain'.[8] Saunders' concept of total pain made the link between these different facets in a way that fundamentally resituates pain, describing it not as a stand-alone element but as something intrinsically interrelated with the 'good death' that Hauerwas suggests needs preparation for. As described below, such pain may be a manifestation of much else, and yet may only come at a time when it is no longer possible to disentangle many of its constituent parts and where healing may prove elusive and partial.

Pain and personhood

Her first description of the term came in 1964, where she described a pain in which 'all of me is wrong', which included physical, emotional, mental and social difficulties contributing to an overall state of pain.[9] Saunders later recognized the limited role of pain-relieving medication in the treatment of this total pain, and stated that 'pain demands the same analysis and

consideration as an illness itself'.[10] In medicine, pain management would become a specialty in and of itself, and yet one
that has not in many ways adopted the insights of Saunders.
Indeed, Hallenbeck and McDaniel, in their review of palliative
care and pain management in the United States, note that while
biopsychosocial elements of pain management are addressed
in later textbooks, 'total pain' is generally not referenced.[11]
While illness is seen as more than a physical disease in such
models, avoiding the 'reductionist conceptualization of illness
that overly stressed biology and neglected more human aspects
of the experience of illness', one of the key elements that was
missing from the biopsychosocial model of illness (of which
George Engel was a key proponent, and which we explored in
the previous chapter) is the spiritual element.

Thus 'Saunders' model seemed to demand an interdisciplinary
approach to understand the problem of suffering', whereas
Engel's approach 'more narrowly focused on the role of psychiatry as a physician specialty' with an 'emphasis ... on the
multidimensional aspects of illness in the *patient* and how
physicians should approach patients using the biopsychosocial
model'.[12] Comparing the two models offers a sharp contrast.
The biopsychosocial model is primarily a model for use,
approaching the relationship between patient and physician as
that between a provider and a recipient. Such a model is focused
on its ends – to provide the most effective (and likely efficient)
clinical encounter. Saunders' model fundamentally reframes
this encounter by a deliberate focus on the human person in
and of him- or herself, rather than as the subject of medical
treatment externally imposed (however sensitively).

Joshua Hordern, focusing on the importance of an appropriate definition of compassion in medicine, favours Saunders'
approach, as might be expected from a theological perspective
that values the individual as a person independent of any subjective position they occupy in a therapeutic relationship. Hordern
uses the imagery of alongsideness and the motif of *peregrinatio*
to describe a 'shared but also journeying nature' of the relationship of people through therapeutic relationships, ultimately a
journey of encounter imbued with meaning for both physician

and patient.[13] The concept of the patient changes. Whereas for the biopsychosocial model the patient retains an element of the 'something', that is, a biological machine, albeit one with a psychology and emotional life, on which medical technique is utilized to some extent, the concept of total pain starts from the idea of the person and moves outwards towards the therapeutic relationship that might be offered by a physician or other therapist. The entity facing the clinician is person first and patient second; pain takes on an existential meaning in and of itself, which is subtly but fundamentally different from understanding it as a biopsychosocial phenomenon.

For Saunders, pain is something that is inhabited by and forms a central tenet of that individual's personhood at that point in time. It may be that the specific field of palliative care (from which she was drawn to medicine[14]), in which patients were frequently told 'there is nothing more we can do',[15] enabled Saunders to approach a patient as an integrated whole in a way that still remains challenging in other parts of medicine today (remaining so in some specialties in which dying is still seen as defeat rather than as integral to medical care).[16] Her Christian faith likewise influenced her self-understanding as physician, seeing her patients as 'beloved' children of God.[17]

Pain and the hospice

Saunders worked within palliative care, a medical discipline that increasingly looks to provide holistic care to those whose disease is no longer curable but whose symptoms might nonetheless be alleviated. Palliative care was previously associated primarily with the care of the actively dying, yet in recent years palliative care has widened to include those whose disease might never be cured and might be 'life-limiting' but may not be life-ending.[18] Nonetheless, such 'life-limiting illness introduces loss into the life of a person and those close to him or her. Grief, broadly defined as the reaction to loss, then permeates their lives.'[19] Such a description and widening of the definition of palliative care is helpful to this inquiry; the concept of total pain is itself useful far beyond the realm of the imminently dying, although to date this has been little recognized across many medical specialities.

Saunders felt that the 'devastating effects' of dying could be ameliorated, as much for the dying as for those left behind, and included within these effects 'spiritual and existential distress', which form part of 'our common humanity'.[20] She saw such an enterprise as fundamental to the caring professions. As someone who practised within, and was a key figure in the development of, the hospice movement (for example the founding of St Christopher's Hospice),[21] Saunders was able to practise, learn, research and redefine as she continued to work – a form of reflective practice and reflexivity that is treasured within the theological academy today.

Saunders held a strong Christian faith, which she more fully developed during her nursing years.[22] The hospice that she founded, like many others, displayed an explicitly Christian ethos, and its Aim and Basis Statement stated:

> Its aim is to express the love of God to all who come, in every possible way ... in the use of every scientific means of relieving suffering and distress, in understanding personal sympathy, with respect for the dignity of each patient as a human being, precious to God and man.

It further described the 'community, united by a strong sense of vocation with a great diversity of outlook in a spirit of freedom', which has echoes of the concept of the communion of saints as developed below.[23] Verhey describes the hospice model as being 'not a contract between self-interested individuals but a covenant and a community', with a 'mantra' of Matthew 25.40, further emphasizing the interconnectedness and personhood of those whom it was set up to serve.[24] Yet 'the dignity of each patient was explicitly recognized (and proselytizing forbidden)', suggesting that even though the hospice itself had an unequivocally Christian foundation, the patients who entered it were seen as autonomous (albeit within a community), reflecting one of the four pillars of modern medical ethics (autonomy, non-maleficence, beneficence and justice).[25] It is arguable that such principles themselves reflect Christian norms.

The narrative of human life

Saunders' life is an example of the falseness of any simplistic dividing line between the secular and the sacred. In many ways, her reflections on the dying and the lack of time and interest given to them by contemporary physicians (reflecting wider society), leading to her developing the notion of total pain – itself developed earlier than the biopsychosocial model[26] – was a theological as much as a medical initiative. Her ability to listen, watch and question what God was doing in the lives of those whom she was treating, and question, from a theological perspective, the structures within which she was working and within which patients were being treated speaks to a deeply reflective and reflexive practice which developed out of an explicitly Christian faith.

She often writes in narrative, telling the stories of patients as people with their own loves, fears, hopes and dreams.[27] It is by not attempting to homogenize this multiplicity of voices but rather in recognizing their 'preciousness' as individuals before God that led to her shifting the ground on which palliative care provision was situated.[28] Saunders' approach differed from the paternalistic model, in which 'the doctor utilizes his [sic] skills to choose the necessary interventions and treatments most likely to restore the patient's health or ameliorate his [pain]',[29] not only in the sensitivity and theological depth she showed towards patients-as-people but also in her conceptualization of their pain. Hers was an approach that saw pain not only as a reductive phenomenon experienced through one particular modality – primarily physical – but one that viewed pain as imbued with meaning for the individual, often a meaning that the individual themselves did not recognize. She described pain as 'not just an event ... but rather a situation in which the patient is, as it were, held captive',[30] and thus moved beyond the common medicalized model, in which physical pain was treated with analgesics, to a position where surprising modalities might be targeted to relieve pain.

An example given in a medical textbook, in which oncological total pain is somewhat reductively described as 'opioid-irrelevant pain' (quoting John Hinton of St Christopher's Hospice), helps illustrate this point. Doctors are informed that 'many of the usual pharmacological measures appear useless, or pain may be relieved in one part of the body only to appear somewhere else'. Patients are found to 'deny any anxiety or psychological distress, but will manifest their distress physically'. The solution is to offer a 'holistic' approach, to avoid the patient (and the family) feeling 'overwhelmed by the experience' with 'no relief'; 'the pain is frequently not "controlled" but "contained", the aim being to achieve the best relief possible without lasting psychological sequelae in those left'.[31] This description reveals the unease that some clinicians show when considering total pain; the almost incidental mention of the patient and the focus on the 'surviving family' is hardly in keeping with modern ideas of person-centred care, and suggests that while a mention is made of 'total pain', the 'biopsychosocial' model is to the fore. The fact that pain in one modality – for example, emotional or spiritual – might be expressed through another (in this case somatic) is a key feature of total pain, and suggests that the modalities of which Saunders speaks (physical, mental and emotional, spiritual, social) appear to be far more closely intertwined than might have previously been thought.

The role of the physician (and other healthcare professionals) in total pain is not about *management* of this pain as such, or at least not as a disjointed primary objective; instead, it is to recognize the integrated (both diachronic and synchronic) nature of the 'beloved' (Saunders' term) and to work from this understanding towards an effective way of navigating an individual's narrative, identifying and addressing the (often multiple) sources, as well as the ostensible manifestations, of the pain. This is subtly different from the description of 'not "controlled" but "contained"' mentioned above. It might be better to describe it as addressing, even if not solving, the pain, and in this case as much for the patient as for the grieving relatives. It is such an addressing of pain that speaks to a wider responsibility of the Christian when living alongside someone with total pain.

'Total pain' and meaning

As we described in the previous chapters, it is not the purpose here to provide a theodicy or to define an ultimate, universal meaning in or through pain per se. However, a key proposition is that specific incidences of pain might themselves have meaning because such meaning may in fact be the cause of the pain. In a reductive form, Dick Millspaugh has attempted to outline the elements that he feels contribute to the spiritual aspect of total pain: awareness of death, loss of relationships, self, purpose and control. He contrasts these with life-affirming and transcending purpose and an internal sense of control.[32] While such a mechanistic, mathematical approach is somewhat unconvincing, nonetheless Millspaugh highlights many of the metaphysical questions and concerns whose lack of resolution – or lack of enunciation, consciously or unconsciously – might lead to pain mediated through different modalities.

It is useful to distinguish between pain that might be 'purposive'[33] and that which is more likely to be an expression of *meaning*. 'Purposive' pain is most frequently seen as a result of acute pain reactions, and is an evolutionary development that ensures an organism avoids maximal damage in a particular situation. Such pain pathways are not always obviously beneficial – for example in the post-operative period or in forms of chronic pain. Clark highlights Saunders' own reflections on this latter form of pain. She recognized it as having the potential of being 'timeless, endless, meaningless, bringing a sense of isolation and despair'.[34]

There is, thus, a fluid relationship between pain and meaning. While 'purposive' pain and forms of chronic pain may have the same initial biomolecular (and evolutionary) basis, their impact on an individual, the person's functioning and sense of self, can be fundamentally different, not least due to cultural or individual differences. While 'total pain' was initially conceptualized as an all-encompassing form of pain that arises *from* a change in a person's self-understanding or existential fears, worries or questions that develop when facing death, chronic, enduring physical (and mental, emotional and spiritual) pain may also lead to such existential elements and a change in the person's self-understanding. It is possible, then, to extend Saunders' definition of total pain not only beyond death and dying but beyond simple unidirectional causalities of pain and meaning that appear to be inconsistent with lived realities. It appears more accurate to describe pain and meaning in a complex dance in which one influences and mediates the other. Indeed, beyond any pain that is solely reflex or short-term in nature, it appears impossible to describe pain without a reference to the meaning such pain has for the individual who is experiencing it – and for the wider community.

Pain that is greater than the initial sum of its parts reflects modern scientific understandings of the interaction between physical, mental and social pain, in which each system interacts with the others and in which are expressed different modalities that may not relate to the initial source of the pain.[35] Saunders' key contribution – in her case a visionary one, made before the delineation of the biopsychosocial model – was to identify pain as residing in a whole person, who is more than the sum of their parts, and who is ultimately not reducible to biomedical processes. This is not necessarily to say that the social, mental, physical and spiritual needs are not mediated through the body, but rather to say that the person's relationship to bodily manifestations is more complex than mere physiological processes – for example, their situation as person-in-community as described below.

Total pain has further implications for the conceptualization of the mind–body relationship. A Christian perspective must ultimately reject the materialistic assumption that 'only the physical is ontologically valid'.[36] Likewise, the concept of Cartesian dualism is rejected both by the scientific understanding of the interrelationship between the mental and the physical,[37] and by the Christian anthropology displayed in the theory of 'total pain'. Total pain links the embodied nature of a Christian anthropology to the importance of the social environment in which we live – in which 'culture plays an important role in the construction of meaning',[38] and in which this meaning plays an important role in the way we experience the world in a bodily fashion. That we are social actors created to live together is foundational to Christian theology; our sense of self involves not only the individual but also the communal. In this conception, the mind is wider than the mere nervous tissue that makes up the brain, even if an individual's mind is ultimately expressed through this.

Any meaning in pain might take a number of different forms. Saunders' prime reflection on the meaning that is causative, at least in part, in total pain is that of loss (and ultimately being alone).[39] In the total pain of the dying, existential questions may be raised in response to the imminent death, the individual recognizing that they are within the 'valley of the shadow of death' (Ps. 23). This recognition may include 'a loss of meaning or purpose, loss of connectedness to others, thoughts about the dying process, struggles around the state of being, difficulty in finding a sense of self, or loss of hope'.[40] There may be guilt and a sense of isolation. The loss being experienced may prefigure the loss seen in death, a loss that may not be immediately less present to those with religious faith than to those without. Those facing chronic illness may also face many of the same losses, albeit to different degrees and with different manifestations.

Purpose, loss and despair

The Hebrew Bible's reference to Sheol speaks to this feeling of loss. 'Sheol cuts a person off from fellowship with God. Those in Sheol cannot praise God or hope in him.'[41] In this understanding, death is in direct opposition to community. It is an 'individualizing' moment, where 'because our narratives are always embedded in the story or world in which we participate', death marks 'an abrupt end to one's personal story'.[42] It is here that the communion of saints and a wider Christian ecclesiology and eschatology may speak to those experiencing total pain, and may offer a corrective – albeit an experienced rather than a pedagogically expressed corrective – to the overwhelming loss prefigured and thus experienced in total pain. Those features described above appear in the end to point to this ultimate loss of connectedness to others.

Frankl, writing after his own experience of the devastation of Auschwitz, describes three sources of meaning as purposeful work, love, and courage in the face of difficulty, each of these possibly different in content from person to person, yet nonetheless similar in nature.[43] It is striking that each requires a recognition of the self in relationship to others, the opposite of the individual being totally alone. For those experiencing total pain, this feeling of or fear of eventually being left alone may come from a number of different sources: fear of death or loss of agency, fear of the loss of friends and acquaintances, fear of losing hope. For the Christian, an antidote to this fear of loss is hope in the resurrection, in the life of relationship at the heart of the Trinity, and in the communion of saints in earth and heaven.

While theological opinion is divided on the meaning of Christ's dying words, '*Eli Eli lema sabachthani?*' (Matt. 27.46 and Mark 15.34), a reading of these words nonetheless suggests that, in his final moments, Christ faced the agonizing fear of loss. An alternative reading might suggest that by quoting Psalm 22, Christ is drawing attention to the fact that he will *not* be lost after death. While it is beyond this chapter's scope to fully develop those arguments, it is important to recognize that such existential questions are situated at the heart of the Passion narrative and thus offer fertile ground for reflection as a Christian community. Whichever is the correct interpretation (if such a thing is possible), it is the debate itself that can aid us in exploring the contrasting shades that are cast on the Passion narrative – in itself, a helpful theological enterprise.

Christ's death on a cross also highlights another element present in the existential questions discussed above – the loss of hope. This loss is perhaps the culmination of the process of losing both meaning and connectedness to others. It may be that the loss of meaning is intrinsically related to the loss of connectedness when viewing the human person from a Christian standpoint. For those in total pain, loss and fear of loss may be so entwined as to be impossible to untangle, ultimately leading to a despair that speaks both to the immediate future and to a wider metanarrative and reflection on one's own sense of being. Despair, perhaps the ultimate destination of such a loss of hope, not only suggests that the individual cannot see beyond the present situation, but that, even more fundamentally, they are beyond any help whatsoever. It is here that loss of hope meets the fear of being totally alone.

A description of the traditional Christian position on despair might be that 'despair paralyses the soul and thus must always be avoided'.[44] Aquinas describes despair as the most deadly of the sins, as 'when hope is given up, men [sic] rush headlong into sin, and are drawn away from good works'.[45] Aquinas associated despair with losing confidence in the mercy of God; if the devil might tempt us to this position, then we might no longer reach for those things that are good and, rather, see no harm in reaching for those that are evil. In Question 20, Aquinas further associates despair with spiritual laziness, in which the soul does not attempt to overcome difficulties but succumbs to them, and thus remains in a state of disorder. He quotes Isodorus in 2 *De Summo Bono* 14 as saying, 'To commit a crime is death to the soul; but to despair is to descend into hell.'[46] As Nohrnberg notes, 'Christianity is partly defined by the hope of salvation, and hope relieves despair. Dante's hell is full of those who are advised to abandon all hope.'[47] The destructive nature and ontology of despair appears to be contrary to the Christian ethic.

Such a position continues to exert influence in the modern era. Kirkegaard, for example, speaks of despair in *The Sickness Unto Death*,[48] describing a variety of levels of despair that lead from despair over the earthly, to despair over the eternal, and ultimately to 'despair to will to be oneself'. At this lowest ebb, the individual 'revels in their own despair and sees their own pain as lifting them up above the base nature of other humans who do not find themselves in this state', a description of those who appear to romanticize the idea of despair, describing it as 'the despair of defiance'.[49] A key gift of the physician-theologian is to examine and investigate individuals as they are. For patients seen by Saunders, despair appears much more likely to develop from a complex web of interrelating stressors than from an intellectualized anti-theism.

Despair may indeed reach this level – a level where despair is over the earthly, the eternal, and even the will to be oneself – yet it appears that a corrective may need to be made to any analysis that describes this as inevitable defiance and not as part of the human experience of extreme or total pain. That the Christian community must seek to alleviate despair through hope may be true;[50] despair itself might not rightly, however, be called 'sin', at least on a personal level. The presence of despair, perhaps, is rather an example of structural sin. The words of Isaiah 42.3 – 'a bruised reed he will not break, and a dimly burning wick he will not quench' – suggest that the community have some responsibility to take on the burden of any such sin (whether despair is complete – which is itself challengeable – or simply *appears* complete), and seek to serve the despairing rather than condemn them.[51] There is a role for the community, or communion, in simply holding the theological virtues of faith, hope and love, in some cases on behalf of the individual in total pain.

Karl Barth, in *The Faith of the Church*,[52] refers back to Christ's death on the cross, stating, 'As soon as the body is buried, the soul goes to hell, that is, into remoteness from God, into that place where God can only be the Adversary, the enemy.' He recognizes that 'our lives too know despair', but not the 'total despair suffered by Jesus Christ alone. This distinction ... ought to keep us from dramatizing our sorrows, however grievous they might be.' Barth recognizes that we may suffer despair, but illustrates the place the Christian community might inhabit, whereby 'we', that is, the Christian community, 'know that Jesus Christ has destroyed the power of hell, however great it may be'. We may truly experience a form of despair as human-kind, yet it is a despair that is, at least in part, impacted by the sufferings of Christ. It is perhaps to this mitigation that the

Christian community might point, in faith and love, offering hope to those whose total pain has overwhelmed them.

Particular medical considerations

At this point, it is important to draw attention to my own situation. I am not experiencing total pain and I am not speaking from a position in which I need to manage such pain. It is my contention that there may be degrees of interrelationship – the dance between meaning and pain – throughout human experience, but the phenomenon of total pain is most likely to be one at the margins of human existence, one identified by dialogue between patients, relatives and clinicians. It is in my role as physician that I am most likely to encounter such a dialogue, and following the example and experience of Cicely Saunders it appears essential that any engagement with those who are suffering such pain is undertaken sensitively and in a narrative fashion. Yet it is also clear that such encounters might prove fruitful in deepening a theological anthropology and likewise a pastoral practice; they suggest a role for the physician-theologian beyond the bounds of palliative care. While total pain might most easily and clearly be seen in that discipline, its dynamics are at play further afield within medical practice.

Those who treat people experiencing total pain may themselves encounter or feel threatened by such pain by transference. Clark again quotes Saunders, who stated that 'The resilience of those who continue to work in this field is won by a full understanding of what is happening and not by a retreat behind a technique.'[53] While resilience in medicine is a contested concept, this once again brings into focus the difference between a biopsychosocial treatment model and the anthropological understanding found in the concept of total pain. Saunders' argument, that only by engaging in such an understanding can resilience be gained, may be optimistic, but it points to the importance of those who treat the sick seeing their work as part of a wider worldview rather than as a group of disembodied techniques. Saunders appears to be arguing that genuine and effective empathy requires an underlying (theological) anthropology for it to be bearable by the treating clinician.

A note of caution might be raised here in relation to mental illness. As we have previously described, for some the loss experienced through the dying process or in the context of chronic illness may lead to what the International Classification of Diseases refers to as either a depressive episode or depressive disorder.[54] Some such people may experience episodes of self-harm or indeed suicide, which themselves may be related to a fear of loss. There is limited literature on the interplay between total pain and depression, and similarly the current understanding of the psychopathology of depression is limited.[55] While some of the insights from this work may play a role in theological approaches to depression, it is key to note that as a recognized discrete illness, which is 'unresponsive to circumstances' and, while primarily relating to low mood, 'may be accompanied by so-called "somatic" symptoms',[56] it would be foolish to assume that a theological anthropology derived from reflection on total pain would give any particular answers to the specific questions raised by depression and other psychiatric illnesses. However, any insights into anthropology may themselves aid in developing a fuller understanding of the person facing loss or perceived loss, and potentially lead to more sophisticated responses to tragic episodes such as suicide than those seen in the history of Christian thought.[57]

In this chapter we have focused on an enhanced phenomenology of the pain experienced as total pain. Such an understanding of pain links the individual with the collective, highlights the interconnectedness of different modalities and the key role that loss plays in the meaning of those experiencing this pain. Understanding the place of the social, spiritual, mental and physical is essential to this enhanced phenomenology – each plays its part and may together lead to a pain greater than the sum of its parts. We will now consider these narratives in the light of the narrative of Christian hope and communion together.

Notes

1 David Clark, '"Total pain", Disciplinary Power and the Body in the Work of Cicely Saunders, 1958–1967', *Social Science and Medicine* 49 (1999), pp. 727–36.

2 Cicely Saunders, 'The Evolution of Palliative Care', *Journal of the Royal Society of Medicine* 94(9) (2001), pp. 430–2; p. 430.

3 Saunders, 'The Evolution of Palliative Care', p. 430.

4 Cicely Saunders, 'The Care of the Dying', *Guy's Hospital Gazette* 80 (1966), pp. 136–42.

5 David Clark, '"Total pain": The Work of Cicely Saunders and the Maturing of a Concept', *End of life studies* (University of Glasgow, academic blogs), 25 September 2014, http://endoflifestudies.academicblogs. co.uk/total-pain-the-work-of-cicely-saunders-and-the-maturing-of-a-concept/#_edn4 (accessed 6.12 2021).

6 Clark, '"Total pain": The Work of Cicely Saunders'.

7 Cicely Saunders, 'Care of Patients Suffering from Terminal Illness at St Joseph's Hospice, Hackney, London', *Nursing Mirror*, 14 February 1964, pp. vii–x.

8 Hayden Ramsey, 'Death Part 3: Our Attitude Towards Death', *New Blackfriars* 86(1004) (2005), pp. 418–24; p. 421.

9 Cicely Saunders, 'The Symptomatic Treatment of Incurable Malignant Disease', *Prescribers' Journal* 4(4) (October 1964), pp. 68–73.

10 Cicely Saunders, *The Management of Terminal Illness* (London: Hospital Medicine Publications Ltd, 1967).

11 James Hallenbeck and Shana McDaniel, 'Palliative care and pain management in the United States', in Rhonda Moore, ed., *Biobehavioural Approaches to Pain* (New York: Springer, 2009), p. 497.

12 Hallenbeck and McDaniel, 'Palliative care', p. 497.

13 Joshua Hordern, *Compassion in Healthcare: Pilgrimage, Practice, and Civic Life* (Oxford: Oxford University Press, 2020), p. 92.

14 David Clark, *Cicely Saunders: A Life and Legacy* (Oxford: Oxford University Press, 2018), p. 75.

15 Stefan Friedrichsdorf, Jody Chrastek and Stacy Remke, 'Supporting transitions: Effective palliative care teams', in Rita Pfund and Susan Fowler-Kerry, eds, *Perspectives on Palliative Care for Children and Young People: A Global Discourse* (Oxford: Radcliffe, 2010), p. 284.

16 Josephine M. Clayton and David W. Kissane, 'Communication about transitioning patients to palliative care', in David W. Kissane, Barry D. Bultz, Phyllis N. Butow and Ilora G. Finlay, eds, *Handbook of Communication in Oncology and Palliative Care* (Oxford: Oxford University Press, 2010), p. 210.

17 Clark, *Cicely Saunders*, p. 137.

18 David Currow and Amy Abernethy, 'Pathophysiology of life-limiting illnesses', in Geoffrey Mitchell, ed., *Palliative Care: A Patient-centred Approach* (Boca Raton: CRC Press, 2008), pp. 36–7.

19 Geoffrey Mitchell, Judith Murray and Jenny Hynson, 'Understanding the whole person: Life-limiting illness across the life cycle', in Mitchell, ed., *Palliative Care*, p. 80.

20 Cicely Saunders, 'The Evolution of Palliative Care', p. 432.

21 Clark, *Cicely Saunders*, p. 145.

22 Clark, *Cicely Saunders*, pp. 44–52.

23 Cicely Saunders, 'The modern hospice', in F. S. Wald, ed., *Quest of the Spiritual Component of Care for the Terminally Ill: Proceedings of a Colloquium* (Yale: Yale University School of Nursing, 1986), p. 45.

24 Allen Verhey, *The Christian Art of Dying: Learning from Jesus* (Grand Rapids: Eerdmans, 2011), p. 61.

25 Tom L. Beauchamp and James F. Childress, *Principles of Biomedical Ethics* (Oxford: Oxford University Press, 2001), p. 12.

26 G. L. Engel, 'The Need for a New Medical Model: A Challenge for Biomedicine', *Science* 196(4286) (8 April 1977), pp. 129–36.

27 David Clark, 'Introduction', in Cicely Saunders, *Cicely Saunders: Selected Writings 1958–2004* (Oxford: Oxford University Press, 2006), p. xv.

28 David Clark, *To Comfort Always: A History of Palliative Medicine Since the Nineteenth Century* (Oxford: Oxford University Press, 2016), p. 89.

29 R. Kaba and Prasanna Sooriakumaran, 'The Evolution of the Doctor–Patient Relationship', *International Journal of Surgery* 5(1) (2007), pp. 57–65; p. 57.

30 Cicely Saunders, 'Nature and management of terminal pain', in Edward F. Shotter, ed., *Matters of Life and Death* (London: Darton, Longman & Todd, 1970), p. 15.

31 Margaret Saunders and Sarah Booth, 'Cancer pain treatment', in Chas Bountra, Rajesh Munglani and William K. Schmidt, eds, *Pain: Current Understanding, Emerging Therapies, and Novel Approaches to Drug Discovery* (New York: Marcel Dekker Inc., 2003), p. 253.

32 Dick Millspaugh, 'Assessment and Response to Spiritual Pain: Part I', *Journal of Palliative Medicine* 8(5) (2005), pp. 919–23.

33 Clark, '"Total pain": The Work of Cicely Saunders'.

34 Cicely Saunders, 'The moment of truth: Care of the dying person', in Leonard Pearson, ed., *Death and Dying: Current Issues in the Treatment of the Dying Person* (Cleveland: The Press of Case Western Reserve University, 1969), pp. 49–78.

35 For further discussion, see Jaak Panksepp, 'The neurobiology of social loss in animals: Some keys to the puzzle of psychic pain in humans', in Geoff MacDonald and Lauri A. Jensen-Campbell, eds, *Social Pain: Neuropsychological and Health Implications of Loss and*

Exclusion (Washington DC: American Psychological Association, 2011), p. 41; Nicholas Hylands-White, Rui V. Duarte and Jon H. Raphael, 'An Overview of Treatment Approaches for Chronic Pain Management', *Rheumatology International* 37 (2017), pp. 29–42; Josianna Schwan, Joseph Sclafani and Vivianne L. Tawfik, 'Chronic Pain Management in the Elderly', *Anesthisology Clinics* 37(3) (2019), pp. 547–60.

36 Jeffrey M. Schwartz and Sharon Begley, *The Mind and the Brain: Neuroplasticity and the Power of Mental Force* (New York: Harper Collins, 2002), p. 28.

37 Stanislas Dehaene, *The Cognitive Neuroscience of Consciousness* (Cambridge MA: MIT Press, 2001), p. 4.

38 John Sanders, *Theology in the Flesh: How Embodiment and Culture Shape the Way We Think about Truth, Morality, and God* (Minneapolis: Fortress Press, 2016), p. 6.

39 Saunders, 'The Evolution of Palliative Care', pp. 430–2.

40 Susan Parker, 'Palliative care', in Karen L. Dick and Terry Mahan Buttaro, eds, *Case Studies in Geriatric Primary Care and Multimorbidity Management* (St Louis: Elsevier Inc., 2020), p. 76.

41 Stanley J. Grenz, *Theology for the Community of God* (Grand Rapids: Eerdmans, 1994), p. 581.

42 Grenz, *Theology for the Community of God*, p. 581.

43 Victor E. Frankl, *Man's Search for Meaning* (London: Rider, 2013).

44 Michael R. Miller, 'Aquinas on the Passion of Despair', *New Blackfriars* 93(1046) (2011), pp. 387–96.

45 Thomas Aquinas, *Summa Theologiae* (Second Part of the Second Part, Question 20: Article 3, Response), translated at New Advent, www.newadvent.org/summa/3020.htm (accessed 12.06.2021).

46 James Nohrnberg, 'Three Phases of Metaphor, and the Mythos of the Christian Religion: Dante, Spenser, Milton', *Spenser Studies: A Renaissance Poetry Annual* XXXI/XXXII (2018), pp. 613–49; p. 631.

47 Nohrnberg, 'Three Phases of Metaphor', p. 631.

48 Søren Kierkegaard, *The Sickness Unto Death: A Christian Psychological Exposition of Edification and Awakening by Anti-Climacus* (London: Penguin, 2004).

49 Gabby McCarthy, *Introduction to Metaphysics* (Waltham Abbey: ED-Tech Press, 2018), p. 191.

50 For example, as discussed in Paul Leer-Salvesen, 'Fear of the future and theology of hope', in Sigurd Bergmann, ed., *Eschatology as Imagining the End: Faith between Hope and Despair* (Abingdon: Routledge, 2018).

51 Ronald Rolheiser, OMI, 'Despair as Weakness rather than Sin', *Angelus* (18 May 2017), https://angelusnews.com/voices/despair-as-weakness-rather-than-sin/ (accessed 12.06.2021).

52 Karl Barth, *The Faith of the Church: A Commentary on the Apostles' Creed According to Calvin's Catechism* (Eugene: Wipf and Stock, 2006), p. 95.

53 Clark, '"Total pain": The Work of Cicely Saunders', quoting Cicely Saunders, 'Current views on pain relief and terminal care', in Mark Swerdlow, ed., *The Therapy of Pain* (Lancaster: MTP Press, 1981).

54 World Health Organization, *International Statistical Classification of Diseases and Related Health Problems 10th Revision (ICD-10) Version: 2010*, https://icd.who.int/browse10/2010/en#!/F32.3 (accessed 12.06.2021).

55 Harvard Health Publishing, Harvard Medical School, 'What Causes Depression?', 24 June 2019, www.health.harvard.edu/mind-and-mood/what-causes-depression (accessed 12.06.2021).

56 World Health Organization, *International Statistical Classification*.

57 Rodney Stark and William Sims Bainbridge, *Religion, Deviance, and Social Control* (Abingdon: Routledge, 2013), p. 12.

4

Saints – friends and companions

The particular theological motif we will bring into dialogue
with 'total pain' is the widely held and central Christian doctrine of the communion of saints. We will begin by examining
its core tenets and asking what implications there are for us as
Christians if we affirm and proclaim the existence of such a
communion in reality rather than only in abstract. We will meet
the saints as friends, guides and companions, as participants in
the sacramental reality of the church and as exemplars of the
relational reality at the heart of the faith. In doing so, we will
find them a necessary and vibrant part of our faith, and one
that has much to say to us in how we conceive of ourselves in
the world, which has implications not only for our theology but
for our practice too.

The existence of the saints in communion

The existence of the communion of saints is professed in the
Apostles' Creed of the universal church, forming a key part of
the inherited teaching of the church catholic. It is thought that
it was first found in a sermon of Nicetas of Remesiana (in the
form of *communio sanctorum*).[1] The veneration (and invocation) of the saints has a long history, often associated with the
early martyrs.

Particular manifestations of this concept were among the key
doctrinal issues contested at the Reformation,[2] and controver-
sies about this teaching remain to this day.[3] In our discussion
here, we must remain alert to the difficulties that veneration
might pose for some Christians, while not losing sight of

the underlying doctrine itself. In recent years there has been increased focus on this doctrine as a unifying one.[4] The thesis of this book is that a renewed interrogation of such a doctrine may also speak to concepts that have been primarily derived outside the explicit realm of 'theology' – for example in the interactions of various disciplines that led to the concept of total pain – and may provide an effective illustration of the Christian worldview that might underlie theological reflection on these ideas.

One of the key dividing lines between Reformed and Roman Catholic understandings of the communion of saints (a line on which side it is not clear the Church of England falls) is the former's rejection of the latter's encouragement to ask for the prayers of the dead. It is useful, however, to consider the Catechism's definition of the communion of saints,[5] as it offers a description of the concept – the living reality – that proves helpful to this investigation. First, it states (para. 946), 'The communion of saints *is* the Church', and further (para. 947), quoting Aquinas,[6] that, 'Since all the faithful form one body, the good of each is communicated to the others ... We must therefore believe that there exists a communion of goods in the Church.' In so doing, the Catechism lays out the fundamental understanding of the communion of saints: that is, it is the church *entire* (living and departed), and there remains by virtue of their inclusion in this body a relationship between each member of this communion. Quoting the Roman Catechism, it described the church as 'a common fund'. The following paragraph of the Catechism makes a conscious link, stating that 'The term "communion of saints" therefore has two closely linked meanings: communion "in holy things (*sancta*)" and "among holy persons (*sancti*)".'

Sacramental living

This is a fundamental point in our inquiry: the communion is not simply a group of people who happen to have become followers of Christ; it is a group who by virtue of being the church share a common life. Since one understanding of the destination of the Christian is the New Jerusalem,[7] such a common life suggests a common journey towards holiness. While there remain differing theological understandings of the Final Judgement and the mechanics of the possibility of redemption after death,[8] nonetheless, by virtue of our place in the church catholic, we form part of the cohort that might best be described as the communion of saints, those who have finished the race and those who remain travelling (2 Tim. 4.7). While the Catechism[9] makes an explicit link with the eucharistic elements as being the holy gifts, referencing 'Sancta sanctis!' in the Eastern rite, this may be too limited an understanding of what these holy gifts – or holy things – may be.

While the eucharistic feast may be the fundamental act of cohesion that defines and conjoins the communion of living and departed, the 'holy things' referred to may have an application that is wider and includes also the experiences, loves, joys and the metaphorical (and metaphysical) food for the journey through Christian life – and death. This interpretation of 'holy things' (perhaps we might also call them 'holy relations') might make explicit the link between the Eucharist as central act of communion – the 'most profound sacramental expression of what it is to be [the] church' – and the *koinonia* of the people of God. Yet such a 'spiritual unity' as discovered in *koinonia* does not stop at the holy table. Instead, both *sancta* and *sancti* are inextricably linked in the communal life of the church, and a free exchange of advice, experience and compassion all contribute to the *koinonia* that is 'a gift from the Spirit' (in Paul's understanding).[10] Such is the communion seen in Acts 2.42, and while the modern church does not practise such a radical distribution of physical goods, it is clear that there is a biblical precedent for a communion of fellowship within the church. Indeed, it appears fundamental that the gifts given by God (Rom. 12.6–8) are for the building up of the people of God, not the individual believer. By virtue of this, the communion of saints is not an abstract theory but should be a lived reality. Debates about the metaphysical mechanics of life beyond the grave should not be allowed to obscure this; it appears fundamental that any Christian narrative includes the existence of the communion.

The Catechism, and St Paul's teaching and the letters of St John (for example 1 John 1.2–3),[11] make an important corrective to any development that might lead to such communion becoming another form of secular communitarianism. Quoting Aquinas, the Catechism states, 'The most important member is Christ, since he is the head', primarily as indicator that 'the riches of Christ are communicated to all the members, through the sacraments'.[12] Paul describes communion as 'first effected in baptism and then further manifested in the Eucharist', which then 'places ethical expectations on members of the Christian community; the freedom proper to believers as followers of Jesus is conditioned by the obligations imposed upon them by their shared *koinonia*'.[13] Philip Sheldrake highlights the specific link in 1 John, where those invited to 'have fellowship with us' are reminded that 'our fellowship is with the Father and with his Son, Jesus Christ'. The communion of saints is a group of people who have been chosen (John 15.16), who have entered into sacramental grace through baptism and whose participation in this communion comes with responsibilities to the other, which in the first instance appears to apply to those within the communion. Such obligations might, however, apply far beyond those bounds, particularly if the message of Luke 10.25–37 is read as a radical reinterpretation of neighbourliness. In such a case, membership of the church – fellowship with God – brings with it a deep and profound obligation to share the holy gifts with one's neighbour, that is, everyone we might meet.

The Catechism's description of this sharing of the gifts, which it calls 'communion in charity' (para. 953),[14] quotes St Paul: 'We do not live to ourselves, and we do not die to ourselves' (Rom. 14.7); 'If one member suffers, all suffer together with it; if one member is honoured, all rejoice together with it. Now you are the body of Christ and individually members of it' (1 Cor. 12.26–27); and '[Love] does not insist on its own way' (1 Cor. 13.5). It here highlights another fundamental facet of the communion, that of 'solidarity'. Here, 'the least of our acts done in charity redounds to the profit of all', yet 'every sin harms this communion'. Solidarity, then, is another way of seeing our membership of such a body: our ultimate good, both individual and corporate, is bound up with the good of all the others in the body. Concepts of structural sin, for example the social sins found in the face of human exploitation,[15] are relatively new within theological discourse, but these ultimately highlight the solidarity found at the heart of the communion of saints. The communion is considered as a single organism with many parts, speaking to the imagery of the body of Christ as found in both Colossians 1 and 1 Corinthians 11. Pain suffered by one member inevitably affects the others. Developing the concept of total pain in this context might suggest that one form of pain or sickness that afflicts one part of the body of Christ may likewise affect the other parts, and the whole too.

The communion of saints might be thought of as a family eating together. This family, however, stretches across time and space, meets under the headship of Christ, and shares in solidarity and responsibility, each member not only contributing to the whole but also participating in and walking alongside the other members, living and dead – the church militant and the church triumphant (and in some conceptions, the church penitent, representing those in purgatory).[16] These concepts of solidarity and responsibility do not remain as such. The doctrine of the communion is not one that remains in the abstract, but rather one that is an eschatological and temporal reality, highlighting the importance of the involvement of the saints in glory. For Christians to profess belief in the communion of saints is to recognize that reality, a reality that is more 'real' than any contemporary worldview or even scientific knowledge. The existence of the communion of saints situates the life of the Christian within a wider narrative of creation, redemption and resurrection; it is a profound challenge to death itself and offers a clear vision of the 'already but not yet' of kingdom theology.[17] Living within the communion is living in both of these realities; it is clear that the role of the Holy Spirit in inspiring and maintaining the communion is key. Abraham Kuyper describes this as 'the rule of Love', stating, 'For what is the communion of saints otherwise than Love in its noblest and richest manifestations? ... the very fruit of the Holy Spirit? ... Love's tenderest and most glorious expression.'[18] The communion is a further gift of God – made most clearly visible at Pentecost.

Kuyper makes a distinction between the church and the communion of saints, highlighting the importance of the church recognizing its need to be coterminous with the communion.[19] He uses a metaphor of the family: a child being born does not know of their relation to the family, thus preventing 'communion between him and the other members of the family'. He compares this to the church, which can 'exist, live, and increase before there is any conscious communion of saints'; thus 'the communion of saints may languish, apparently disappear, yea, even be turned into bitterness'. He describes the church as 'the body', with the communion as 'its support and nourishment', which is 'invisible and unknown ... on earth part of the tenor of the faith, and which in the New Jerusalem shall be turned into a rich and blessed experience'. He also makes clear that 'this rich and comprehensive confession may not be belittled by a narrow conception' that speaks of only 'a communion of a *few* saints', which is 'by no means *the* body of Christ'.[20] The communion of saints must therefore be far wider in space and time than any particular Christian community – indeed, it may expand beyond professed Christians to all those who have 'fellowship with God'.

Communion as fellowship

That the communion permeates through all the ages and is yet ever present, most particularly at the eucharistic altar, is routinely declared in the prayers of the church and reflected in words of scripture. Found in Eastern and Western canons, the words that precede the consecration of the elements during the Eucharistic Prayer often take a similar form to those in the Book of Common Prayer:

> Therefore with Angels and Archangels, and with all the company of heaven, we laud and magnify thy glorious Name; evermore praising thee, and saying: Holy, holy, holy, Lord

God of hosts, heaven and earth are full of thy glory: Glory be
to thee, O Lord most High. Amen.[21]

This prayer is situated at the heart of the most sacred prayer
of the church and suggests that the 'company of heaven' (that
is, the church triumphant) join in with worshippers in praising
God during the Sanctus hymn (originally found in Isa. 6.3). It
is the communion of saints, with the order of angels, that are
gathered together at this particular moment in time to sing the
praises of God, and that are frequently referenced in the book
of Revelation. The communion is both outside time and space,
and yet has particular manifestations within it, most clearly
seen during the act of Eucharist. This reflects the importance
of the Eucharist as seen in the Catechism; the Eucharist is the
sacrament that most embodies the communion, a communion
that is drawn together (at least in part) by those entering through
the other dominical sacrament, that of baptism.

Other great hymns of worship in the church universal express
belief in the existence of the communion of saints, including the
Te Deum,[22] which itself might be described as a hymn of the
communion. The continuity between church and communion
is clearly seen, as is the paradox that declares the inadequacy
of human conceptions of time and space and yet also declares
the centrality of the historical events of incarnation and resurrection. Here, too, is seen the orientation of the communion
towards Christ as head: the apostles, prophets and martyrs
'praise thee', and 'all the earth doth worship thee'.[23] This highlights the key Christological motif that is found throughout
discussions of the communion: the communion is a communion
solely because of their fellowship with God (through the life,
death and resurrection of Christ, with Christ as their head).

Ephesians 4 is a key text in which the body of Christ and the
communion of saints reaches a level of definition. Here again
it is 'Christ's gift' of grace (v. 7) that 'equip[s] the saints for the
work of ministry, for building up the body of Christ, until all
of us come to the unity of the faith and of the knowledge of the
Son of God, to maturity, to the measure and the full stature of
Christ' (vv. 12–13). Paul makes it clear that it is by grace that

the communion of saints is breathed into being, and the 'all of us' suggests that Kuyper's point that the communion is the 'nourishment' for the church on earth is key. It is through this nourishment that the communion can 'promot[e] the body's growth in building itself up in love' (v. 16).

Paul's correspondents are now 'citizens with the saints and also members of the household of God, built upon the foundation of the apostles and prophets, with Christ Jesus himself as the cornerstone' (Eph. 2.19–20) – an interesting continuity being highlighted between the apostles of the New and the prophets of the Old Testament. The community becomes part of 'the whole structure', which is 'joined together and grows into a holy temple in the Lord' (v. 21). They take their places among the saints because of the grace through Christ, and because they were 'created in Christ Jesus for good works, which God prepared beforehand to be our way of life' (v. 10). In becoming saints, they sit under Christ, 'the head over all things for the church, which is his body, the fullness of him who fills all in all' (Eph. 1.22–23). This is a remarkable passage, in which is found a very high view of the communion of saints as being the 'fullness' of Christ by virtue of being 'his body'. Forming part of this fullness, the Christian 'can no more fail to take … interest in each other's welfare, than the hand can fail to sympathize with the foot'; 'the success of one is the success of all', and 'each must pray for all'.[24] It is an intentional reciprocity and solidarity that is once again highlighted in this high calling, one for which the Christian is equipped through the grace of God.

Hebrews 12.1 likewise refers to the reality of the communion, describing 'so great a cloud of witnesses'. It is interesting that the preceding passage has referred to the heroes of the Jewish faith who are these witnesses, again highlighting the tension between the Christological shape of the communion and the inclusion of those who did not profess faith in Christ. This speaks perhaps to a level of overflowing grace from Christ the cornerstone (Eph. 2.20), who was 'in the beginning with God' and through whom 'all things came into being' (John 1.2–3). However, it is also the language of 'witness' that is particularly interesting. Those called to be saints are urged to 'lay aside every weight and the sin that clings so closely' because of the cloud of witnesses that surrounds them. This lends significance to the ever-present nature of the communion, acting not only in solidarity but also as witnesses to the actions of those they are journeying alongside. Such witnesses can cajole and encourage, hold up a mirror to sin and also point to hope. The communion is ever present, a living and constant reality whose members are in dialogue and in dynamic relationship, which holds each of us to account and yet also offers a hand when we stumble. It is in this light that asking the prayers of the saints in heaven perhaps makes most obvious sense.

The doctrine is a declaration of belief in a community in which the resurrection is a lived reality. The communion only carries weight as a concept when it is genuinely lived, and for this to be so, the life in Christ beyond death is an essential component. In the era that the phrase was added to the Creed, 'it is evident that ... the consciousness of communion with the redeemed in heaven ... was as real and as rich in hope to the theologians as to circles of ordinary Christians'.[25] In this period, solidarity was expressed with the martyrs during the act of consecration of the Eucharist, which would take place on an altar associated with their relics.[26] It is therefore entirely in keeping that the communion of saints, far wider than the particular gathering of the church at any specific celebration, be considered present at the Eucharist. There is a clear association between a celebration of the Eucharist in a specific place and time on earth and a corresponding taking of this celebration into the heavenly banquet, most clearly seen in the *supplices te rogamus* of the Roman Canon:

> command that these gifts be borne by the hands of your holy Angel to your altar on high in the sight of your divine majesty, so that all of us, who through this participation ... may be filled with every grace and heavenly blessing.[27]

The communion and not only the local community are gathered at the Eucharist.

Communion in devotion and prayer

'*Communio sanctorum* was first believed implicitly and practised devotionally – almost instinctively – before it was confessed explicitly and handed down in the creed.'[28] As such, the communion set the backdrop to the self-understanding of the early Christian communities, which in DeLorenzo's terms, 'proclaims the permanent validity of the humanity of Christ and the real, historical efficacy of the Incarnation'. Quoting Rahner, he states:

> because the heart of the Christian faith is the Incarnation of the Word of God, who was not merely 'at one time of decisive importance for our salvation ... he is *now* and for all eternity the *permanent openness* of our finite being to the living God of infinite, eternal life.'[29]

It is here that the paradox of the inadequacy and yet importance of time and space meet. DeLorenzo quotes Rahner summing up this position, in which the concrete points to the eternal, and where '*communio sanctorum* at once indicates the unsubstitutable particularity of holy persons, their communion in Christ through the Spirit, and the bonds that unite them':

> When the Church declares someone to be a Saint, this is much more a necessary part of the Church's realization of her own being ... she must be able to state her holiness in the concrete. She must have a 'cloud of witnesses' whom she can indicate by name. She cannot merely maintain that there is a history of salvation (without it being known exactly where it takes place with real, final success), but she must *really relate* that very eschatological history of salvation which she is herself.[30]

Such a belief in the concrete particularity of individual saints, and in a communion in which the innumerable are nonetheless counted by God, contributes to an understanding of the alongsideness of the communion. For some, engagement with the communion may refer to specific named people, for example saints whose names are taken at confirmation or ordination. For others, the more ephemeral notion of a 'cloud of witnesses' may prove more helpful – although with the necessary corrective that the communion is not an abstract proposition. This concreteness can prove beneficial when considering those participants in communion who remain alive, or are yet to be born. Exploitation, unwillingness or inability to know of or prevent harm to others we do not know (either through space or time constraints) are significant human evils, and recognizing others as particular children of God and co-heirs with Christ (Rom. 8.17), rather than as abstract statistics, might lead to a kinder Christianity – or, rather, a kinder church. DeLorenzo describes this position as 'relating to particular persons bonded together in communion',[31] stressing the importance and inextricability of communion and personhood.

As we have stated, controversy remains about the validity of asking the intercession of the saints, and the validity of praying for the dead. As co-sojourners on the journey towards the final culmination of the world (even were we to accept that the Final Judgement had already occurred upon death, and that some have been permanently excluded from the communion, or that some wait beyond death for that Final Judgement[32]), it seems impossible to reconcile the core Christian doctrine of the communion with a total refusal to recognize the dead as active and present parts of the communion. At worst, it appears to be in direct contradiction to what is said in scripture about the communion and the body of Christ, a communion in which the holy of all ages are united. Karl Barth, perhaps, puts forward a moderate Reformed position:

> I am not so sure that the saints of the Church are unable to come to our aid ... yet one fact is certain: that neither the living nor the dead can be for us what God himself is to us ... a help in that great distress which is ours in the face of the Gospel and the Law.[33]

Barth rightly situates any doctrine of the communion of saints in the light of the orientation towards God; it is because of this fellowship that the communion exists, and it is nothing if it is not oriented in this way.

If we are to understand the communion as entailing the holy through all generations, then it appears entirely appropriate to expect from, and expect to offer to, these persons-in-community: one of these 'holy things' must surely be intercession. As a fundamental activity of the Christian, prayer must infuse any communion-based relationship – whether that is being prayed for, offering prayers for others, or praying (and praising) along-side others, as described in the Canon, the Sanctus and Te Deum above. This being-alongside others leads to another dimension of the communion, that of an extended and extending group of friends and family in Christ.

Friends and companions

Donald Bloesch suggests that the communion of saints is not only 'solidly anchored in Scripture' but also 'a potential source of comfort to the church militant in its trials and struggles'. To cement this point, he quotes the Reformed theologian Pierre-Yves Emery, who links this comfort to prayer: 'We are truly surrounded by the prayers of the saints; we are the object of their love, and efficacious love because it is incorporated in prayer.'[34] That friends might sometimes carry our hope, our fears, our joy, our excitement, even our belief, is something experienced in our daily life; to consider the communion of saints as an extended group of friends adds a richness to this vicariousness. As Scott Hahn states, 'we are never alone. We need never be afraid. This is a simple corollary of our salvation.'[35] Saints are a gift of friendship from God, a gift that embodies his friendship in love (John 13.34–35; John 15.12–15). As members of that communion, the individual Christian is both gift and the one gifted to. In the saints, Christ himself calls at the door and knocks (Rev. 3.20); and likewise, whatever is done to one of these, it is done to Christ (Matt. 25.40).

St Anselm writes of his 'saint-friends', who he 'hopes ... will triangulate his relationship with God, their friend'. In addition, 'loving others and forming friendships in the world, as impenetrably distant as friends may be, nonetheless mimic the behaviour of God and win merit in His eyes', suggesting that for Anselm the very action of developing friendship itself brings one closer to God.[36] He 'understands himself through the lens of the Redemption as a potential self, a capacity for God ... which, although always in flux, strives to return to its origins as a stable image of God'. It is through friendship with the saints that Anselm can 'realize ... his identity in relation to God and God's love'.[37] Anselm finds himself through these relationships, through a 'longing for spiritual unity' among the saints.[38] He wishes to 'enter "more deeply into the fullness of the people of God, where he talks with Christ and the saints as a man talks with his friends"'.[39] Such friends might prove to be better companions than those met on earth, for reasons outlined below.

Anselm felt that Christ 'did not quickly die a salvific death on the cross; instead He lived among people for a long time, became their friend, and then, beyond His death, extended that friendship to the saints as well'.[40] This is of fundamental importance, and here Anselm might disagree with Barth, arguing that friendship with the saints could 'bridge the gap between Christ and the human sinner' and thus the friendship itself 'assumes ... a healing power through which the individual has ... a chance to appeal and pray to God because the saintly friends intervene on his behalf and become the crucial intermediaries'.[41] Anselm argues that friendship with saints − ultimately an indirect way of reaching God − may itself prove better than direct relationship. McDonie considers the possible justifications for this and notes that 'since the saints had been human, they would be capable of understanding the sinner's frailty and need of help', and could thus intercede for the sinner on earth − the friendship itself being an extension of the work of God. Indeed, 'Anselm even turned toward the saints' shortcomings and failures in their lifetime to build a bridge to his own human experience in order to evoke sympathy' − what McDonie describes as 'sympathetic identification' − and hoped that the saints might be able to share some of their 'overflowing' goodness with the sinner on earth.[42] Anselm is making friendships both to feel able to stand before God and also, in the relationships themselves, to attempt to overcome his failings, at least to some degree. The communion of saints is as much a gift to the sinner on earth as it is a community and is there for the sojourner on earth to lean upon.

Communion as relationship

Barth builds on the concept of the *imago Dei* that is found in Anselm's writing, which for Anselm is both a 'source of lament ... because the divine image in him is so damaged and darkened by sin that he must be reformed and recreated for it to carry out its proper function', and also an 'occasion for Anselm's gratitude, because it enables him to think of God, love God, and know God'.[43] While Barth's argument is not that the saints act as intermediaries, he nonetheless recognizes that 'we are most fully ourselves as we live with and for our neighbours' – what Cambria Kaltwasser helpfully describes as our 'co-humanity'.[44] Because God has 'created us for mutuality with our neighbours, God's command that we live with and for one another aptly "interprets" our lives', ultimately leading to a form of interdependence and a rejection of the 'pure' self.[45] This need to be in communion with neighbours complements the ideas of Anselm about the importance of saint-friends triangulating our relationship with God.

Indeed, it is because we are born for relationship (in Barth's view) that such triangulation is so successful. While Barth and Anselm approach the question from different angles, both are similarly positive about the role of the neighbour in revealing the truth not only about the human person, and our specific human person, but also about the *imago* that is within us. The idea that relationship is at the heart of God is fundamental to Trinitarian theology, most particularly seen in the social trinitarianism of theologians such as John Zizioulas.[46] Our own need for and ultimate flourishing in communion may be a reflection of the perichoretic nature of God Godself. For Barth this Trinitarian element is fundamental: his concept of 'co-humanity' is located 'not just in Christology but in the eternal life of the Godhead'.[47]

Life lived in relationship requires effective reciprocation and an acknowledgement of the subjectivity of the other. In Barthian terms, 'I contradict my humanity every time I try to live as though my neighbour did not exist', which suggests a train of thought similar to that developed in the work of Martin Buber.[48] For relationship to be key to the human and divine life, the 'other' must be fully recognized as such, and yet the self must recognize its own need for the communion to be fully realized as 'self'. The communion ultimately emphasizes both the individual and the corporate, one requiring the other in order to be most fully defined. Only those who recognize the subjectivity of the other can bless them; likewise, only those who recognize the other can be themselves blessed. The communion of saints is the concrete, lived demonstration of this subjectivity; it is only within the communion of saints that any individual, living or dead, can truly live the Christian life, as this is the outpouring of relationship that ultimately nourishes the body of Christ.

The communion of saints provides the fount of relationship that accompanies the individual Christian on the journey towards the New Jerusalem. This journey, it appears, may continue beyond death, and given the inevitable impact of encounter on both persons in a relationship, those journeying *in via*, whether alive or dead, must make an impact on each other. This, perhaps, offers a glimpse into how and why those who have died might still be changed, even once their life on earth is over. This is the ever-increasing growth in holiness, a growth that can no more be ended by death than can life, and that leads ultimately to perfection, confirmation, strengthening and establishment in Christ (1 Pet. 5.10).

Not only is the holiness of the individual built up, but the holiness of the body also. Referring to the saints, DeLorenzo notes that 'the unique particularities of these holy persons were, each in their own way, conformed to and transformed by the love of God in Christ', which 'is impossible in isolation'. He links this growth in holiness back to the Holy Spirit, which 'is the communion of the Father and the Son given over to the world'. Indeed, the communion of saints 'at once indicates the unsubstitutable particularity of holy persons, their communion in Christ through the Spirit, and the bonds that unite them', each of which builds up the other in holiness. 'That which makes these particular persons holy is precisely that which forms them into one communion.' It is of the nature of God and his communion with creation that the holiness is developed in this way. If pain (and its association yet not total elision with suffering[49]) is to some extent culturally mediated, then the making present and visible of the communion of saints, with all its theological implications for loss and despair, must surely be part of the role of the church militant.

We have found the communion not only to be foundational to the Christian life but have identified the several roles that the saints might play. The saints might be our guides, friends, confidantes or advocates, our witnesses, educators, chiders and encouragers, our travelling companions, our extended family, our vicarious supporters, our worshipping community, our port in the storm and our vision into the life of God in communion. We now turn to ask how our doctrine of the communion of saints might yield further implications for our present enquiry, by considering how that doctrine is situated within the wider sweep of Christian doctrine.

Notes

1 A. T. Hanson, 'Communion of saints', in Alan Richardson and John Bowden, *A New Dictionary of Christian Theology* (London: SCM Press, 2002), p. 114.

2 Martin Luther, 'Sermons on the Catechism, 1528', in John Dillenberger, ed., *Martin Luther: Selections from His Writings* (New York: Knopf Doubleday Publishing Group, 2011), p. 212.

3 Gill Goulding, 'Reformation and Recusants: Christian Unity and the Communion of Saints', *Pro Ecclesia: A Journal of Catholic and Evangelical Theology* 26(1) (2017), pp. 49–55.

4 For example, in Bilateral Working Group of the German National Bishops' Conference and the Church Leadership of the United Evangelical Lutheran Church of Germany, *Communio Sanctorum: The Church as the Communion of Saints*, trans. Mark W. Jeske, Michael Root and Daniel R. Smith (Collegeville: Liturgical Press, 2004).

5 The Vatican, *Catechism of the Catholic Church* (London: Bloomsbury Academic, 2002).

6 Thomas Aquinas, Symb. 10, as quoted in The Vatican, *Catechism of the Catholic Church*.

7 Ellen F. Davis, 'Teaching the Bible confessionally in the church', in Ellen Davis and Richard B. Hays, eds, *The Art of Reading Scripture* (Grand Rapids: Eerdmans, 2003), p. 21.

8 Jerry Walls, *Purgatory: The Logic of Total Transformation* (Oxford: Oxford University Press, 2012), p. 43.

9 The Vatican, *Catechism of the Catholic Church*, p. 224.

10 Philip Sheldrake, ed., *New SCM Dictionary of Christian Spirituality* (London: SCM Press, 2013), ebook 'Communion/*Koinonia*'

11 Sheldrake, ed., *New SCM Dictionary of Christian Spirituality*.

12 The Vatican, *Catechism of the Catholic Church*, p. 217.

13 Sheldrake, ed., *New SCM Dictionary of Christian Spirituality*.

14 The Vatican, *Catechism of the Catholic Church*, p. 224.

15 Gregory Baum, 'John Paul II on structural sin', in Gregory Baum, *Essays in Critical Theology* (London: Sheed and Ward, 1994), p. 189.

16 The Vatican, *Catechism of the Catholic Church*, p. 954.

17 George Eldon Ladd, *A Theology of the New Testament: Revised Edition* (Grand Rapids: Eerdmans, 1993), pp. 66–7.

18 Abraham Kuyper, *The Work of the Holy Spirit*, trans. Henri de Vries (New York: Cosimo, 2007) p. 548.

19 Kuyper, *The Work of the Holy Spirit*, p. 549.

20 Kuyper, *The Work of the Holy Spirit*, p. 549.

21 Church of England, 'The Lord's Supper or Holy Communion', www.churchofengland.org/prayer-and-worship/worship-texts-and-resources/book-common-prayer/lords-supper-or-holy-communion (accessed 12.06.2021).

22 Encyclopaedia Britannica, 'Te Deum laudamus', www.britannica.com/topic/Te-Deum-laudamus (accessed 12.06.2021).

23 Church of England, 'The Order for Morning Prayer', www.churchofengland.org/prayer-and-worship/worship-texts-and-resources/book-common-prayer/order-morning-prayer (accessed 12.06.2021).

24 Charles Hodge, *A Commentary on the Epistle to the Ephesians* (New York: Robert Carter & Brothers, 1856), p. 392.

25 Jaroslav Pelikan, *Credo: Historical and Theological Guide to Creeds and Confessions of Faith in the Christian Tradition* (New Haven: Yale University Press, 2005), p. 396.

26 Enrico Mazza, *The Celebration of the Eucharist: The Origin of the Rite and the Development of Its Interpretation*, trans. Matthew J. O'Connell (Collegeville: Liturgical Press, 1999), p. 225.

27 Catholic Academy of Liturgy, *A Commentary on the Order of Mass of the Roman Missal* (Collegeville: Liturgical Press, 2011), p. 250.

28 Leonard J. DeLorenzo, 'Belief in the Communion of Saints Isn't Optional', *Church Life Journal* (2 November 2017), https://churchlifejournal.nd.edu/articles/belief-in-the-communion-of-saints-isnt-optional/ (accessed 12.06.2021).

29 DeLorenzo, 'Belief'.

30 Karl Rahner, 'The church of the saints', in Karl Rahner, *Theological Investigations: Volume 3*, trans. Cornelius Ernst (Limerick: Mary Immaculate College, 2000), pp. 93–6.

31 DeLorenzo, 'Belief'.

32 Donald G. Bloesch, *The Last Things: Resurrection, Judgment, Glory* (Downers Grove: InterVarsity Press, 2004), pp. 35–6.

33 Karl Barth, quoted in Bloesch, *The Last Things*, p. 37; original reference is Karl Barth, *Prayer*, trans. Sara F. Terrien (Philadelphia: Westminster Press, 1952), p. 20.

34 Bloesch, *The Last Things:*, p. 37; original reference is Pierre-Yves Emery, *The Communion of Saints*, trans. D. J. Watson and M. Watson (London: Faith Press, 1966), p. 111.

35 Scott Hahn, *Angels and Saints: A Biblical Guide to Friendship with God's Holy Ones* (New York: Image, 2014), p. 23.

36 R. Jacob McDonie, 'Mysterious friends in the prayers and letters of Anselm of Canterbury', in Albrecht Classen and Marilyn Sandidge, eds, *Friendship in the Middle Ages and Early Modern Age* (Berlin: Walter de Gruyter, 2010), p. 314.

37 McDonie, 'Mysterious friends', p. 313.

38 Gavin R. Ortlund, *Anselm's Pursuit of Joy: A Commentary on the Proslogion* (Washington DC: The Catholic University of America, 2020), p. 214.

39 Ortlund, *Anselm's Pursuit of Joy*, p. 214, quoting Benedicta Ward, 'Introduction', in Anselm, *The Prayers and Meditations of St Anselm with the Proslogion*, trans. Benedicta Ward (London: Penguin, 2006) p. 52.

40 R. Jacob McDonie, 'Mysterious Friends in the Prayers and Letters of Anselm of Canterbury', p. 314.

41 McDonie, 'Mysterious friends', p. 134.

42 McDonie, 'Mysterious friends', p. 135.

43 Ortlund, *Anselm's Pursuit of Joy*, p. 107.

44 Cambria Kaltwasser, 'Karl Barth on what makes us human', The Thread: Princeton Theological Seminary, https://web.archive.org/web/20181213141708/https://thethread.ptsem.edu/culture/karl-barth-on-what-makes-us-human (accessed 14.02.2023).

45 Kaltwasser, 'Karl Barth'.

46 For example, John Zizioulas, *Being as Communion: Studies in Personhood and the Church* (Yonkers: St Vladimir's Seminary Press, 1985).

47 Joseph L. Mangina, *Karl Barth: Theologian of Christian Witness* (Louisville: Westminster John Knox Press, 2004), p. 96.

48 Mangina, *Karl Barth*, pp. 95–6.

49 Smadar Bustan, 'Diagnosing human suffering and pain: Integrating phenomenology in science and medicine' in Simon van Rysewyk, ed., *Meanings of Pain – Volume 2: Common Types of Pain and Language* (Cham: Springer Nature Switzerland, 2019), pp. 46–50.

5

Participating in Christ – the narrative of communion

At this stage, it is worth our taking a step back and asking two things: first, does our belief in the doctrine of the communion of saints mean anything to us in practical terms? Does it actually impact us? Second, is this belief consistent with, and does it interact with, our wider Christian theological understanding? These two things are not unrelated, most particularly because the Christian faith is a faith that makes claims not only about what we do but also about who we are, in the widest sense of that phrase. The created world, our sense of selves and purpose, the ways we think and act, all of these can, on occasion, end up appearing in direct contradiction to one another, whether we recognize this or not. For the theologian, however, it is essential that, even if we are unable to form a full systematic theology (and whether we should aim to do so is itself a moot point), we must nonetheless have coherence, both within our 'thought' theology and between our 'thought' and 'acted' theology. As we have discussed in Chapter 1, this is by no means a unidirectional conversation.

We will address the practical – and further anthropological – consequences of our belief in such a doctrine as we turn to Part 2. For now, we will focus on the second of these questions: how does this doctrine engage and sit within the wider ecosystem of Christian doctrine? In doing so, we will think first about the history of the doctrine itself and discover some of the different ways it has fed Christian anthropological understandings across time and traditions. We will then return to our themes of relationship, fellowship and participation, and ask what insights we might glean from other elements of Christian doctrine that might encourage us to believe that the communion of saints has something to say that is therapeutically and soteriologically significant not only for the sufferers of 'total pain' but for all of us who recognize its presence in our midst.

Communion as gift – The Hiroshima Report

Before we delve into some of the historical understandings of communion as it directly relates to the communion of saints, it is worth spending some time considering the different meanings and understandings given to the concept of 'communion' as it is. The word 'communion' may refer to a number of different elements of the Christian life, and in so doing it forms a visible link between them. We might think, therefore, of 'Holy Communion', the Eucharist (itself meaning thanksgiving), of a communion of believers as a description of an institution (in the Anglican case, the Anglican Communion), or of a spiritual reality (for example in the phrase 'we are in communion with one another'), and the communion of saints is an example of this latter meaning. The word communion is, therefore, associated with themes of faith, fellowship, sacramentality and thanksgiving, all held within a spiritual reality. Communion not only has a number of meanings but – while perhaps intangible and various – it does refer to something that 'is'. It is not an abstraction.

Because of this, it is essential that church leaders and theologians are careful about how the word is, and is not, used, and whether our definitions of communion are true to its form. Obvious disagreements can be cited in this area, particularly as they relate to the different meanings of the Eucharist. However, it is also important to recognize that phrases such as 'impaired communion'[1] or 'separated' communion,[2] for example, say something about what we believe the nature of communion to be. This is not, in itself, problematic, but it is key that such definitions are fully explored, together with their implications. It is, perhaps, for this reason that there has been a recent increase in interest in this area in ecumenical affairs.

A key report here is The Hiroshima Report, Koinonia: *God's Gift and Calling*, which came out of the International Reformed–Anglican Dialogue (2020).[3] This report describes communion in clear and unambiguous terms:

> We believe *koinonia* is grounded in [the] life of the Triune God, in which we are invited to participate together. *Koinonia* is God's gift for the life of the Church, to be lived out responsibly in God's world.

This statement, which is deceptively simple, contains within it very clear themes. Communion (*koinonia*) 'flows out of the interpersonal life of the Trinity',[4] and the life of the Trinity is something in which we are invited to participate. Communion is, therefore, found within the nature of God; it is not incidental to our wider doctrine, but rather springs from it and is found at its heart. It is an invitation to us to participate, and is a gift to the life of church. It is 'communion, fellowship, sharing, participation, and partnership ... sharing together in a reality that is greater than ourselves and our own individual needs'. It is a term fundamental to the theology, ecclesiology and missiology of the church and found throughout scripture, rooted in worship and the sacraments. It 'leads to fellowship and dialogue', 'has an eschatological dimension', 'frames a missiological understanding of God's world as interconnected and interdependent', and ultimately 'encompasses accountability and responsibility for one another and all of God's creation'. Fundamentally, 'the social and moral dimensions of *koinonia* require life-giving stewardship of God's gifts'.

It is clear from this document that the here-and-now, earthly, social and relational elements of communion cannot be easily separated out; they are intrinsic to any understanding of the concept. Communion is not a mere definition of a doctrine – it cannot be defined without it being enacted. It is scripturally based and essential to the life of the church, not only because it flows from the Triune God but because it is gift. This fundamentally resituates any discussion we might have of communion and of ownership over it. Communion becomes something given rather than something we might place boundaries around. As such, communion becomes a matter of participation, yet not only a participation in the life of the church but also a participation more widely in the life of God. It is no longer possible to draw a neat line that divides the two: they are both intimately associated one with the other, and inseparable.

We have considered some of the scriptural resonances of communion in the previous chapter. A key text that links the life of communion with the life of the Triune God is 2 Corinthians. Here we find (2 Cor. 13.13), in the NRSV translation, the use of the word 'communion' itself returning into use: 'The grace of the Lord Jesus Christ, the love of God, and the communion of the Holy Spirit be with all of you.' The NRSV also offers 'and the sharing in' as an alternative for 'and the communion', which highlights the absolute association of communion with the Holy Spirit – something to be shared in, or participated in. The Hiroshima Report describes this as overflowing 'from the beautiful and holy truth of God, who is Father, Son, and Holy Spirit – love and grace in relationship', which 'manifests the personal interconnectedness of perfect unity and difference in abiding and caring community'[5] – the 'new creation' of 2 Corinthians 5.17. The Report goes on to implicitly link this outpouring of Trinitarian 'love and grace in relationship' with 'the fundamental unity of the Body of Christ'. Communion is 'as complex and multidimensional as the Church itself',[6] and yet is the ultimate truth found at the heart of the Christian church.

As 'gift, given to the Church by the grace of the Holy Spirit', *koinonia* becomes explicitly pneumatological in nature; and hence communion itself appears to be part of the nature of God. The Hiroshima Report suggests that 'the *koinonia* that is expressed within the community of the faithful flows from the dynamic vibrancy of the divine *koinonia* into the self-giving of the Church for the good of all creation', suggesting that 'as the three persons of the Trinity are distinct and yet exist in perfect unity', the church too 'is many, yet one body'. In doing so, it makes explicit the link between the *koinonia* within and flowing from the Godhead. It is not necessarily clear, however, as to whether these *koinonia* are one and the same or whether the communion between believers is reflective rather than substantively the same as the communion in the Godhead. Nonetheless, it is clear that – as gift – *koinonia* is not something that can be disregarded by those wishing to live in Christ, to participate in the creative life of the Triune God. *Koinonia* is, then, fundamental to who we are as Christians.

Koinonia and the communion of saints

If we take the vision of 'love and grace in relationship' as our understanding of communion, our first question is to ask whether this is the communion we might find displayed in the communion of saints. In other words, does our definition of the communion of saints adequately reflect this wider understanding of the nature of God and of the gift of God to live the Christian life? If it does reflect this reality, then we must surely recognize the necessity of the communion of saints as part of living the life that God has given to us. The communion of saints is no longer only necessary because of its role in the church – it is necessary too because it speaks of, and is itself 'of', the nature of God and God's relationship with humankind.

If we apply *koinonia* to our understanding of the communion of saints – an entity of solidarity and companionship across time and space – then we recognize some clear and unambiguous consequences for our life together, which will include our life together as those in pain and those who do not suffer pain but nonetheless form part of the community. The Hiroshima Report tells us that *koinonia* is 'irreversible and unbreakable at the extremes of both divine self-emptying (*kenosis*) and human suffering'.[7] It is seen in scripture as 'the gift [that] continues to draw people into new relationships of transformation even when it appears to be mortally threatened'. This kind of understanding strengthens the importance of this doctrine when considering total pain, for sufferers and for those in solidarity alike. While human companionship and friendship might appear to be breaking, this is a proclamation of the unbreakability of the communion of God and of God's saints. Despite possible appearances, life lived in communion is a life that shows that 'love is strong as death' (S. of Sol. 8.6).

Love and communion are surely deeply related, both in terms of the out-working of communion and in its fundamental conception as being part of the nature of the Godhead. The Hiroshima Report addresses the first of these, which is highly applicable to our conception of ourselves as part of the communion of saints:

> As a sign and servant of God's design for the world, the Church lives into its calling and being as *koinonia,* and offers itself as a community of compassion and justice shaped by the love of Christ for and with the world.[8]

We might go further than this. While it is certainly true that the church on earth might find *koinonia* to be one of its attributes, we must surely address the question from the other direction: the church has 'calling and being as *koinonia*' because the church on earth is part of a *koinonia* that is bigger than the church on earth, and is found most fully expressed in the communion of saints. This is not to reduce the importance or the need for the visible representations of this communion to be 'a community of compassion and justice', but it is to remind ourselves, as we saw in the last chapter, that the communion of saints helps us to resituate the church as we see it within a much broader conception of the church 'as it will be'. It is clear that even 'the communion of saints' is, in a sense, incomplete; its numbers and composition will surely increase until the end of time.

The Report itself is one that focuses on ecumenical matters, and thus is understandably concerned with the life of the church and churches as much as institutions as spiritual realities. Yet it does seem fundamental that we regain an understanding of the church on earth as something that is part of a wider reality. The Report's key point of narrative – that *koinonia* is gift – is surely an excellent tool in achieving this. Indeed, a focus on the communion of saints as gift might also be a helpful ecumenical starting point, as it helps free conversation from the worldly and aims rather towards an ecumenical understanding that speaks not of institutions but of a spiritual reality that finds its anchor in the Triune God.

The communion of saints across time and place

Having reviewed a recent ecumenical understanding of the doctrine, it is worth reviewing how the communion of saints has been understood in different times and places. In *A New Dictionary of Christian Theology*, A. T. Hanson quotes Gregory the Great as having given justification for the practice of invocation of the saints as follows: 'The saints inwardly see the brightness of Almighty God, and therefore we cannot believe that they are ignorant of anything outward (*Moralia in Job* 12.12).'[9]

It is clear from this that, in the seventh century, the reality of the ongoing life of the saints was not seen as entirely separate from the life of the church on earth, and it appears to suggest that the saints themselves are acutely aware of life on earth. This being the case, it may be that asking for the prayers of the saints is not so much prevailing upon them to notice something happening on earth, or to bring their attention to a particular concern, but intentionally to join ourselves with them in a form of solidarity, a solidarity from which we can benefit not least because the saints 'inwardly see the brightness of Almighty God' and thus pray with a knowledge not yet given to those on earth. The saints' prayers may not be any more 'efficacious' (an unhelpful term), in that they may not bring about more by their action, but that is also surely a fundamental misreading of the role and mechanics of prayer. The Church of England suggests that:

> To pray is to make our hearts ready to experience the love of God in Jesus Christ through the power of the Holy Spirit … Prayer opens us more deeply to the transforming grace of God. We enter into God's presence, allowing the Holy Spirit to pray in us.[10]

This being so, the saints' prayers might themselves be more 'effi-cacious' because, by gazing on the 'brightness of Almighty God' and holding the concerns of earth in this light, they are more perfectly aligned with the will of God ('thy will be done on earth as it is in heaven'). Returning to the role of the Holy Spirit and of the communion of saints as an expression of pneumatology, it is perhaps the saints in heaven whose prayers are most closely those of the Holy Spirit. It may be that in invoking the prayers of the saints (who, as per the Council of Trent (1545) 'reign together with Christ'),[11] what we are truly doing is desiring that our prayers, too, might be more conformed to the life of the Spirit, and in being so, our lives might be more conformed to the life of Christ.

A not dissimilar point is made when considering that vener-ation of the saints formed part of the practice in the time of Cyril of Jerusalem (fourth century AD). Hanson quotes Max Thurian as stating:

> There is a theological necessity to recall the saints in the liturgy of the Church. They are a reminder of the mediation of Christ in the universal Church of all time. The Son of God has willed to be present in the incarnation to men by the mediation of his humanity. The risen Christ has willed to leave certain signs which recall and realize this mediation ... The saints are therefore the signs of the presence and of the love of Christ ... It is thus that in the ancient Church prayer for the apostles, prophets, and martyrs became after their death a prayer with them in the communion of saints on behalf of the whole Church.[12]

This suggests a not dissimilar understanding of the communion of saints that we have seen throughout these two chapters, and yet situates it clearly within the liturgy of the church, emphasizing the importance not only of the doctrine but of its proclamation. Seen here, too, is the sacramentality of the com-munion of saints. The saints are 'the signs of the presence and of the love of Christ', which we might build upon by suggesting that the existence of this communion is not a sign of but is the actual outpouring of the life of the Trinity. Yet the existence of signs is significant in itself, a visible reminder of the mediation of Christ 'in the universal Church of all time'. We see an implicit understanding that the 'once for all' incarnation event is nonetheless somehow made present for each generation. Returning to the theme of the last chapter, it is interesting that this sign is so clearly associated with liturgy, and in particular eucharistic gatherings, where the whole communion is brought into mind, whether through sight or through signs. At the Eucharist, the risen Christ is remembered and made present; at the Eucharist there is 'a theological necessity' to recall the saints, too, and in so doing reveal them as 'signs of the presence and of the love of Christ'.

We see here an understanding of 'prayer with' the saints 'on behalf of the whole Church'. The saints are not merely interceding 'for' but also 'with', as is found in some liturgies: 'Let us ask the saints to pray with us and for us.'[13] The element of solidarity and fellowship remains, and appears part of the 'theological necessity' and therefore taken as read. The reality of the saints praying with us is thought of as no more unusual than praying with others in the daily prayer of the church. The living and the dead are not different in essence in this understanding, even if they might be different in their orientation to beholding the face of God.

It is perhaps worth considering the challenge that this doctrine can present to modern scientific understandings at this point. So far, we have identified that the early church – and the church today – saw the existence of and prayer of the dead as somehow present and contemporaneous to their own prayer. This presents two challenges, the first of which was touched on in the previous chapter. We briefly considered the variety of views on death in the first and previous chapter, but it is important to recognize that there are a number of different theological strands that may not agree on what occurs after death, even were eternal life to be accepted as an embodied (in some sense) reality.[14] While it is not possible to do justice to the whole gamut of different understandings, it is fair to say that the majority of Christian theologians would agree that there is some kind of differentiated existence post death (frequently described as embodied, in that individuals retain some sense of individual existence, albeit one defined by relationship with the divine).

However, our understanding of the mechanics of salvation – the way in which judgement is meted out and salvation (or otherwise) assured – is by no means agreed, even within denominations.[15] As we discussed in the previous chapter, the communion of saints nonetheless requires there to be some relationship between the dead and the living, and it is almost certainly reductive for us to refuse to recognize this based on a human understanding of the space–time continuum. Released from such strictures, we can also answer the second of the challenges, that from the secular world, which might view our belief in some form of consciousness beyond death in the form of the church penitent and triumphant as impossible to reconcile with the passage of time or our understanding of astronomy and physics. In essence, any attempt to try to trap the biblical imagination within the human brain – that is, any attempt to tie the message and meaning of the gospel into our own readings of scripture – will end up falling short. The communion of saints is a gift and impetus to opening our minds to understandings beyond this limited vision.

The communion as integral to Christian doctrine

We have spoken about *koinonia* as gift, and about how our doctrines and experiences might interact with one another. One particular gift that this doctrine might give us is to resituate our understanding of scripture and of the world within a worldview that takes as a given that our current scientific understanding of the world is both essential (as we see in our treating of, for example, acute pain) and also contingent. It is contingent in two ways. First, it is contingent in that science is always pushing towards greater understanding and is always keen to disprove itself in service of further knowledge. Christians have spent far too long being opposed to science out of fear and discomfort.

We must not see a belief in a Christian theological worldview as being implacably opposed to science, or we shall find ourselves in the same place as those who, in denying evolution, tied the life of the church to what was – in essence – outdated science.

Yet a belief in the communion of saints does also make a scientific worldview contingent in another sense, by arguing that such a worldview does not necessarily encompass everything there is in human existence. Even were we to understand all there is to understand about the natural world, that would not necessarily give us the tools to answer questions about human experience that sit outside that sphere of competency. It is here that New Atheism often falls apart; it is easy to explain much in terms of science, but when asked to explain the 'why' of certain human experiences, we are unable to do so.

That is not to say, in any way, that science, discovery and human knowledge cannot contribute to our understanding of the world or of human experience. Scientific discovery may challenge our doctrines and lead to refinement and further interrogation, as we discussed in the Introduction. But it is to say that we need not adopt a reductionist worldview to see science as a human good. Science is surely a gift of God, but it doesn't negate the reality of the gift of the communion of saints. These two things are not in conflict.

It is perhaps this conflict with a reductionist scientific perspective, and faith in the living God of Abraham, Isaac and Jacob, and the incarnation, death and resurrection of Jesus Christ as a historical and yet transhistorical event, that makes Christianity both an attractive faith and one that requires the imagination to step beyond having all the answers. Some Christians attempt to use scripture in a similar way to natural science, hoping that the Bible will yield up answers to questions in the same mode as science. What the communion of saints – and pain, as we have previously discussed in Chapter 2 – do is to demand we re-adopt the lens of mystery in what we proclaim. The communion of saints is not an easy, unpackable doctrine, or one that readily yields to the 'how' of scientific explanation. That does not mean that we have nothing to say about it – something that this book has, hopefully, convinced the reader of! But it is to say that the questions we ask of Christian doctrine are different in nature from those in natural science, while at the same time stating with absolute certainty (in faith) that something – in this case the communion of saints – is.

The point of faith is that it cannot be proved. It can be argued for in its totality as part of an argument for Christian theological thought, but once we look for proof we are making use of the wrong tools. To return to our discussion of pain, the questions that we are asking here are those of meaning. The communion of saints is a manifestation of meaning, an answer to a question about who and why we are who we are. How we understand the communion of saints, then, is a question of definition: we are not competent to ask questions of its mechanics of existence, but it in turn does ask questions of us. In other words, it defines us rather than the other way around. Our key question here – one to which we must surely say 'yes' – is whether the communion of saints is an essential part of our doctrine or otherwise. Revelation tells us it is so. We can choose to believe or otherwise, but, as we have shown in this chapter, it is not adiaphora (a thing indifferent), as it is central to our underlying doctrine of God. If it is not, then we must somehow remove it from Christian thought, and the test of such an endeavour would be the vision of God it leaves behind. It is not at all clear that we can lose this *koinonia* without losing something of the essence of the Triune God. As a doctrine it is, at heart, how we as Christians understand what it is to be human and, as such, its interaction with concepts such as total pain (itself a mixture of scientific and theological thinking) is not optional.

Communion as social reality

Before considering the ultimate implications of this argument, let us briefly consider again why the connection of the communion with Trinitarian life is so key. The Trinitarianism of Jonathan Edwards is instructive in this domain. Edwards speaks of the 'society' of the Father, the Son and all believers (the 'household' of God), who share such a relationship through communion in the Holy Spirit.[16] It is beyond the scope of this chapter, but while debates continue as to whether his Trinitarian theology was following a social model of the Trinity, it is clear that the Holy Spirit is that in which connection is found. Krister Sairsingh, in Bezzant's *Jonathan Edwards and the Church*, outlines his understanding of Edwards' theology:

> Since the love which binds the Trinity together is the same love which binds the church to the Son and the saints to each other, we can rightly conclude that the structure of relationship which constitutes the glory of God or God's internal fullness is the same structure which constitutes the reality of the church ... the re-presentation of the societal and relational structure of God's trinitarian life in the community of the saints is, in a manner of speaking, the visibility of God in the world.[17]

We have previously commented on the role of the communion as sign, but in this conception the communion moves beyond sign, in that its 'visibility' is the 'structure of relationship which constitutes the glory of God', a relationship of love which itself 'binds the Trinity together'. As Bezzant comments, 'The divine glory ad intra and ad extra, expressed in the Son and through the Spirit, is a model of order and not of confusion, appealing to philosophical rigor and not superstition, visible in God's work in the church.' The love found within the communion is of the essence of God, and in this reading the existence of the communion is therefore entirely consistent with the reality of the Trinitarian God. It is 'the same love' that binds all together, and hence the communion of saints is a participation in God the Holy Trinity.

Danaher describes the twofold participation in the Holy Spirit as vertical, where 'the saints interpersonally participate in the Godhead through the indwelling of the Holy Spirit', and horizontal, 'where the saints experience friendship and communion with each other on the basis of this shared goodness and love'. He further quotes Edwards as stating (in *Miscellanies* 211) that 'the word *koinonia* in the New Testament connotes not only one's individual incorporation in the life of the God-head, but the "common partaking of the Holy Ghost with other saints"'.[18] In making this explicit, Edwards ultimately leads us into an understanding of the absolute necessity of such a twofold life in the Spirit. The communion of saints therefore has Trinitarian as well as eschatological and ecclesiological implications; according to Edwards' conception, the two are inseparable. This surely has significant implications for our life together as Christians and suggests an innate sociality to the Christian life.[19]

Communion as soteriology

Edwards offers us, too, a further insight into the role of the communion in our life as Christian disciples, and an associated reflection on wider Christian doctrine. As Amy Platinga Pauw argues, 'As both the means of incarnation and the means of the ontological transformation of the saints, the agency of the Holy Spirit is at the center of the work of redemption.'[20] This being the case, we must surely consider further the soteriological implications of the communion of saints.

The Hiroshima Report states that 'the activity of the Triune God is most perfectly revealed in the gift of creation and in the life, ministry, death, and resurrection of Jesus and in the out-pouring of the Holy Spirit', and describes koinonia as being a central theme throughout the life of Christ (it is 'fundamentally given in creation and renewed uniquely in Christ'). The Report argues:

> The cosmic reconciliation effected through the cross and resurrection reveals that at the very moment *koinonia* appears to be broken (e.g. Jesus's cry of dereliction, the tearing into two of the veil of the Temple, etc.), a new richness and fresh unity is being unveiled.

Not only is a link implied between the importance of *koinonia* and the life of Christ, but there is a suggestion that a refusal to break *koinonia* is found at the heart of the salvific working of God. The report makes this point explicit by suggesting that 'this communion is the irreversible achievement of Jesus's cross and resurrection, confirming the permanence of God's reign into which all are invited'. *Koinonia*, then, is both a sign of the reign of God and as an entity appears to be directly affirmed by the salvific events of Calvary and the empty tomb. *Koinonia* is not broken despite Christ's death, Christ is 'the agent of a restored koinonia for those who come to him':

> Through sharing this *koinonia*, those who proclaim Christ's death and resurrection become one Body for worship and mission. This points to the corporate salvation, which sees the embodiment of the divine perfection of humanity in a community of faith, the Body of Christ. As sign and servant of the coming Kingdom that Body becomes sacramental, as Christ is the ultimate Sacrament through whom the full riches of God's promises for the whole of creation are known and realized.[21]

This is an extraordinarily rich passage, which situates *koinonia* centrally within the life of the church as both sacrament and as the lifeblood of the body of Christ, which must surely include those living *and* departed (although the report does not make this explicit). The essential link between *koinonia* and the life of Christ is also striking in the use of the phrase 'corporate salvation', linking the acts of God with the 'community of faith, the Body of Christ', which is 'the embodiment of the divine perfection of humanity'. The inescapability of the relationship between the communion of saints and the redemptive acts of God becomes even clearer, as does the 'worship and mission' that is engendered by such an association. The communion of saints is no longer merely an entity to which one belongs, but rather a life-force that propels the body of Christ to act. Considering this impetus in the light of Edwards' insights above about the Holy Spirit, we find our link with the ongoing work of ushering in the kingdom of God. Sociality is not incidental, therefore, to the work of salvation and participation in the life of the Kingdom of God.

Communion as social participation

We have discussed the centrality of the doctrine of the communion of saints to issues of Trinitarian and soteriological theology, but it is important to identify its role in the creative and redemptive will of God as a participatory one. This participation appears to have an intentionally social element, and is one that is the work of the Holy Spirit – the communion finds its role in the love that is its lifeblood. It is notable that the doctrine of the communion of saints includes each of the theological virtues among its key attributes: it is a communion entered into by faith, a communion that speaks of the future culmination of all things in hope, and a communion that is fed and watered by love. Our relationship to one another as participants in the communion is a relationship that reflects – and springs from – the love of God.

We have spoken above of the unbreakability of this communion, beyond and despite death – both of Jesus Christ and of our own human lives. As we have said, this may appear counter-intuitive to us now, but belief in its truth has been a consistent feature of Christian discipleship. Cyprian of Carthage, in the third century, stated:

> Let us remember one another in concord and unanimity. Let us on both sides [of death] always pray for one another. Let us relieve burdens and afflictions by mutual love, that if one of us, by the swiftness of divine condescension, shall go hence first, our love may continue in the presence of the Lord, and our prayers for our brethren and sisters not cease in the presence of the Father's mercy.[22]

Over time, it may be that the apparent feasibility (and certainly the immediately obvious nature) of such a belief has become lessened, and it is perhaps a challenge for Christians in the twenty-first century to continue to profess this belief. Yet it remains fundamental to Christianity – ultimately a faith that is described in terms of relationship, within the Godhead, within humanity, between the divine and the human, and in the power of the Holy Spirit. The importance of relationality in many modern societies has reduced, with increased loneliness and isolation. It may be that the communion of saints is a way for the church to talk to society afresh.

In their book on Jonathan Edwards' theology, McClymond and McDermott point out his intense engagement with the social elements of life beyond death. In the first instance, he argued that 'an expectation of reunion [with departed believers] was no remnant of pagan superstition but an integral part of the Christian hope' (basing his belief on St Paul's epistles to the Thessalonians). 'God not only resurrected individual saints. God resurrected societies of saints. God resurrected relationships.' As they suggest, 'Edwards' account of heaven exhibited his irreducibly social vision of human life.'[23]

Edwards' belief in relationship continuing post death is one that we might do well to reflect on in modern society. Funeral eulogies will frequently include statements about 'meeting again', but it is by no means clear that a simple connection can be made between relationships on earth and those beyond death. Yet our practice does suggest that we pray to particular saints, and as we found in these two chapters, Christian doctrine does recognize some individual existence post death (the 'eternal life' of the Nicene Creed), a life that might more perfectly express the *imago Dei* that is imprinted on us all and to which we are called. Questions on this topic are significant, from the nature of embodied existence, to personality, to longevity (or otherwise) or intimate relationship, and must all be addressed in the light of scripture and our understanding of Christian doctrine.

What the doctrine of the communion of saints offers us, perhaps, is a renewed opportunity to reflect on what individuation-in-community might look like in terms of our current and future life in the communion of saints, in a shared and common life. This has a significant impact both pastorally and theologically. Although beyond the bounds of this book, we might reflect on it as we consider the conversation between 'total pain' and this most central of doctrines. It is to that conversation that we now turn.

Notes

1 Anglican Communion News Service, 'Anglican provinces declare "impaired" or "broken" relationship with ECUSA' (9 December 2003), www.anglicannews.org/news/2003/12/anglican-provinces-declare-im paired-or-broken-relationship-with-ecusa.aspx (accessed 10.11.2022).

2 Joseph Ratzinger, *Meaning of Christian Brotherhood* (San Francisco: Ignatius, 2013), p. 98.

3 International Reformed–Anglican Dialogue, The Hiroshima Report, Koinonia: *God's Gift and Calling* (2020).

4 The Hiroshima Report, p. 7.

5 The Hiroshima Report, p. 12.

6 The Hiroshima Report, p. 14.

7 The Hiroshima Report, p. 15.

8 The Hiroshima Report, p. 22.

9 A. T. Hanson, 'Communion of saints', in Alan Richardson and John Bowden, eds, *A New Dictionary of Christian Theology* (London: SCM Press, 2002), p. 114.

10 Church of England, 'Learning to Pray', www.churchofengland. org/prayer-and-worship/learning-pray (accessed 02.12.2022).

11 Thomas Scannell, 'Intercession (Mediation)', in Charles George Herbermann et al., eds, *The Catholic Encyclopedia Volume 8* (New York: Robert Appleton Company, 1910).

12 Max Thurian, *The Eucharistic Memorial: Part II, the New Testament* (London: Lutterworth Press, 1961), p. 23.

13 For example, in my home parish of St John the Divine, Kennington, where the prayers end 'Let us ask our Lady to pray with us and for us to her son, Hail Mary ...'

14 As discussed previously, there is an excellent discussion in Bart Ehrman, *Heaven and Hell: A History of the Afterlife* (New York: Simon and Schuster, 2020).

15 Interesting, too, is the lack of a doctrine of purgatory in Eastern Orthodox understandings, and yet the existence of a de facto practice of praying for the dead. The late Metropolitan Kallistos Ware outlined the position, stating, 'Of course we do not understand exactly *how* such prayer benefits the departed. Yet equally, when we intercede for people still alive, we cannot explain how these intercessions assist them. We know from our personal experience that prayer for others is effective, and so we continue to practice it.' Kallistos Ware, *The Inner Kingdom* (Yonkers: St Vladimir's Seminary Press, 2020), p. 36.

16 Jonathan Edwards, 'Miscellany 571', in Ava Chamberlain, ed., *The Works of Jonathan Edwards, Volume 18, The 'Miscellanies'* (New Haven: Yale University Press, 2000), p. 110.

17 Rhys S. Bezzant, *Jonathan Edwards and the Church* (New York: Oxford University Press, 2014), p. 66.

18 William J. Danaher Jr, *The Trinitarian Ethics of Jonathan Edwards* (Louisville: Westminster John Knox Press, 2004), p. 95.

19 While beyond the scope of this chapter, this point might be further discussed in the light of the work of Dan Hardy and Dietrich Bonhoeffer on sociality and life in community in the context of the communion of saints and its inextricable link to a relationship with God.

20 Amy Plantinga Pauw, *'The Supreme Harmony of All': The Trinitarian Theology of Jonathan Edwards* (Grand Rapids: Eerdsmans, 2002), p. 146.

21 The Hiroshima Report, p. 16.

22 See www.newadvent.org/fathers/050656.htm (accessed 10.02.2023).

23 Michael J. McClymond and Gerald R. McDermott, *The Theology of Jonathan Edwards* (New York: Oxford University Press, 2012) p. 307.

Part 2

6

Talking pain with saints

The communion of saints is perhaps the key to the fulfilment of Irenaeus' *Gloria Dei vivens homo* (the Glory of God is a living man), as the phrase goes on to say 'and the life of man consists in beholding God'. This beholding of God is done by living in Christ and by recognizing that we are 'part of the vibrant, even visceral, display of the creation itself'.[1] Beholding God – living in fellowship with him and recognizing oneself as part of the created order, and most particularly the order of the saints through all time and space – is a glimpse of what living in Christ means for the Christian. As we have seen, the communion of saints also has distinct pneumatological and Trinitarian implications; the beholding of God is done through and because of the life of the Spirit as the lifeblood of the communion. The beholding of God is part of the participation in God and the life of God. It is to the implications of such 'living' for the concept of total pain that we now turn.

Caution must be observed, however, in suggesting that any particularly theological approach might provide immediate relief for any individual at any particular point in time. A key facet of total pain is that the pain arrives and arises from a number of different dimensions – the communion of saints is not a simplistic way of 'rising above' pain, or an attempt to tell the sufferer that things are not so bad and thus should be moved beyond. It is also not an attempt to theologize the pain away, or to seek spiritual relief for all aspects of total pain. It is, though, to take seriously the whole-person nature of total pain, and to affirm this within the whole-person-in-communion reality that the doctrine proclaims.

A holistic anthropology

It is also to proclaim something fundamental about the underlying and defining anthropology that we are led to through our
belief in such a doctrine. Such a proclamation is important not
because it seeks to offer simplistic answers or 'sticking-plaster
faith', but rather because a resituating of our self and corporate
understanding in such a doctrine has both theological and practical implications that can help shape Christian communities
into places that are better able to respond to total pain, both
that of the individual and the community more widely. It is,
ultimately, about laying the ground for life lived more closely to
the heart of God – and in the Spirit. Our ability to engage with
'total pain' is, in a sense, a by-product of this, and yet an intentional focus on it here enables us to see in lived-out terms what
such a doctrine might require of us, and how life as experienced
might refine that doctrine too.

Saunders argued for what we have called an 'enhanced phenomenology' when viewing and treating total pain, taking the
individual as entire, not in part, recognizing total pain as an
expression of a number of different, inter-linking pathways. This
can be extended further when considering that not only is the
human being's 'being' more widely interpretative than merely
biological, but that being is also one that is best expressed, and
best understood, as one in communion. Such a step, which
necessitates a Christian worldview that looks to Christ as the
head of this communion and which takes seriously the existence
of such a communion and the individuality and essential nature
of each part of that communion (1 Cor. 12), means that even
an enhanced phenomenology that approaches the individual as
being greater than the sum of their parts still fundamentally
misunderstands humanity if it does not recognize the need for
relationship in the Spirit. Total pain is not solely that suffered
by the individual: it is a social phenomenon, as human beings
themselves are social phenomena. For the Christian, that sociality ultimately finds its definition and understanding in Christ,
and, as members of Christ's body, the total pain of one must in
necessity affect all, through all ages. When one member suffers,

the whole body suffers. We return, then, to the fundamental importance of sociality in our life together.

As we have seen, humans express their pain in social terms (and vice versa), through meaning, language and other phenomena that relate to sociality.[2] John Milbank posits that Augustine holds that 'virtue cannot properly operate ... except when collectively possessed'.[3] The same must be true about those things that break down as well as build up a society. If individuals in the communion of saints are experiencing pain in an existential way, then this suggests more needs to be done to interrogate and identify its cause and its nature, and then look for remedy, if such exists. We might think, too, about what 'properly operating' pain might look like, how a society or individual might find their pain held in a context in which the communion is a lived reality. Of course, this will of necessity remain contingent, and yet it is not something that is dispensable if we are to live in 'properly operating' communion. This has implications for our pastoral and liturgical practice, language and common expression of meaning – in other words, our expressions of 'properly operating' Christian sociality-in-communion.

Pain from the margins

Total pain is not a comfortable idea or presence for society. It disrupts our human narrative of 'success' and speaks of fear and loss to a culture that would prefer to keep these things far from view. Those who experience a pain that remains in some way on the margins of what society considers acceptable may find themselves marginalized – and even excluded – from that society. In the previous chapter, we reviewed the work of the International Reformed–Anglican Dialogue in the Hiroshima Report,[4] which focuses primarily on the concept of *koinonia* as the foundational gift of Christian life together. This report makes special mention of those excluded by society, not as an act of 'charity' but because of the nature of communion itself. As they state, 'The call of *koinonia* is to act justly ... [which] entails courageous participation in life-affirming action in and for humanity and all of creation.' This communion 'is not abstract but is experienced in particular lives and situations', and 'compels us to see and embrace those who are most in need':

> Within societies, there are multiple 'centres' of power and many who are pushed to 'margins'. Those in the centres often have their rights, freedoms, and individuality affirmed and respected, while others are excluded from justice and dignity. Threats to life are particularly acute for those on the margins. That any person or community would be relegated to margins is itself an indication that *koinonia* is distorted and has yet to be fully received.

Those in total pain must surely include those 'on the margins', and hence not only does life in the light of the communion of saints have something to say to them but they also reflect something of the brokenness and 'distortion' of the *koinonia* of the whole when they are marginalized and ignored. This, of course, is a statement that relates to elements of human suffering and marginalization far beyond total pain, and yet it is without doubt that those in total pain are often scapegoated or ignored and seen as too difficult to engage with by Christian communities and even theologians. Blithe and well-meaning statements about the importance of hope do not address the realities of total pain; instead, they silence the experiences of those who suffer. In so doing, they do not proclaim a strengthened Christian doctrine but a weakened one. Total pain does not disappear by being ignored.

Those experiencing total pain often appear locked away – in hospitals, with therapists, shamed into avoiding polite company or overwhelmed with blame and feelings of worthlessness simply because of the pain.[5] Such shame and worthlessness may, as we have described, be associated with a form of scapegoating by society at large. Those facing these existential questions do so so that others don't have to (which may also extend to dynamics of self-exclusion and undesirability). The Beatitudes (Matt. 5.3–12; Luke 6.20–23) suggest that such people hold a particular place in the love of God, even if they are experiencing deep hurt; they suggest that such people, who have not 'already received your comfort' may be bearing prophetic witness to society. In the case of the communion of saints, the presence of fear – in its various forms – that underlies total pain must be taken very seriously indeed. As demonstrated in the works of René Girard,[6] scapegoating is incompatible with membership of God's own company, the saints.

The way that we choose to address the societal (and social) brokenness that leads to scapegoating is also important; it is not merely the addressing but the method that speaks of living in communion. This is key, because living in the light of this doctrine is not simply about providing pragmatic and practical answers (even though there may be an element of this found within our response) but about an entire resituating of our self-understanding. Living in communion will require us radically to review whether the way we currently live as Christians and as Christian communities truly reflects our underlying self-understanding. Yet this, too, is not enough. If we are to live in the world (if not 'of' it), then we must see that the living out of our doctrine also requires our engagement with the world as it is (returning to our discussions of the Five Marks of Mission in our Introduction). The communion of saints is not something that speaks only to Christian community – it speaks to the world in its entirety. This may not readily be received, but nonetheless we must surely find ways to argue for this understanding of human life, not only from a theoretical-theological perspective but also seeking practical change in the world as we participate in the Spirit-filled communion of God. This, of course, lies at the heart of true mission: an engagement with the world that is neither solely theological nor practical, but elides the two into a wider way of being that showcases the out-workings of our theology.

The Hiroshima Report reminds us that this is not an act of human creativity but rather a pro-creative act, a participation in God's creative will. '*Koinonia* is not an expression of charity from the powerful to the powerless', but a 'manifestation of communion with God, humanity, and all of creation'. Communion is not ours to somehow spread or create; it is something that is revealed and gifted by God, as something that is not our property but a gift that is given to all of humanity – and, we might argue, all of creation – equally (albeit, with different implications throughout the created order). There are different implications of communion for each of us. Those of us with privilege, in this case those of us for whom total pain is not a lived reality, and in particular those of us who are called to practise the art of healing as doctors and other healthcare professionals, must surely have a greater responsibility to call for recognition of the reality of the communion of saints, with the pastoral implications this will have.

The Hiroshima Report goes further on this point:

> In contrast to prevailing social patterns, in life together in *koinonia* the experiences and perspectives of people on the margins are valued, lifted up, and considered transformational for the whole. This is a profoundly important theological insight; it is not simply an incorporation of marginalized persons into existing systems and structures. Those at the margins become witnessing agents of life-transforming *koinonia*.[7]

In the light of total pain, therefore, we might argue that not only should these individuals not be hidden away, but their 'experiences and perspectives' should be actively 'valued, lifted up, and considered transformational'. This may seem like a form of legitimization by the privileged, but in fact it is simply a (long overdue) recognition of their legitimization by God. Our task, then, as Christians and specifically as theologians is to identify the 'life-transforming' *koinonia* to which they point, and then to resituate our own self-understanding in this light. This demands that we include such people as equal conversation partners and meet them on their own terms, rather than those that we – or wider society – determine are appropriate. It may also suggest that our pastoring *to* them might be shaped best by a mode of listening rather than the temptation to provide answers that might make us feel more comfortable and built up but might break down the communion of which they are 'witnessing agents'.

We are ultimately called to recognize the *imago Dei* in them *to the same degree* as it is in us, even if the mystery of suffering (both internally felt and in part externally mediated by a society that wishes to hide them away) might impact on their own feelings of connectedness with the divine. While this concept may be applicable more generally to others who are marginalized by society (Christian and secular), those in total pain present a further challenge, in that those suffering total pain may be in despair, experiencing a loss of sense of connectedness with the divine (of course, it is possible that other groups who are discriminated against may feel the same, but in this case it is part of the definition of 'total pain', and thus takes on a particular meaning).

Our understanding of communion demands, however, that despite this loss we affirm their *imago* and do not condemn them as having 'lost hope' as some form of active decision on their part. We affirm (we must affirm as part of our life together) their belovedness despite their hopelessness, and we must then ask ourselves what this tells us about our communion and about the God who is reflected within it. This affirmation is not the stuff of easy answers and may make little difference to that individual, and, in fact, if issued blithely and without any accompanying action, may be little more than lukewarm words. Yet that affirmation tells us something fundamental about ourselves as Christians and as part of the communion of saints – and it tells us something about that communion as well.

It is – at the very least – a corrective to theologies that show a reliance on the individual's felt sense of belovedness, or on their intellectual assertions. It is, too, a corrective to theologies that focus so heavily on individual and personal salvation that the corporate is forgotten. Here we see that the individual and the corporate are far too closely linked for this focus to speak effectively to the human condition. This is not to say that the receptiveness of an individual has nothing whatsoever to do with their salvation, but it is, perhaps, to suggest that their place in communion has more to offer to our understanding of soteriology than we previously recognized to be the case. It is also to suggest that God's authority is not challenged by those things that disturb us most, even existential fear.

Fear and loss

Such fear is not often welcomed by the world, in which success, youthfulness and control are widely heralded.[8] Yet for Christians, this world is not the end – in either meaning of the word: yearning after these short-term and ultimately futile goals appears to be entirely wrong. However, these aims are sometimes seen woven into the theology of 'ultra-modern, energetic, and upwardly mobile' – sanitized – church cultures.[9] The presence of total pain is a challenge to this, suggesting that there are members for whom this form of 'success' is unattainable. The despair felt may be due to inappropriate yearning for this very success, whether through errant theology, through worldliness or through the impact of a wider culture that may claim itself to be inspired by Christianity. Yet the very fact that such despair is present is a reminder to those who, for now, can blithely remain worldly: their experience is but part of that of the communion from which they get their meaning. For the 'successful' to simply ignore the despairing is a grave error, particularly when they are but part of Christ's body; it denies the universality of Christ and hence the communion of saints. A communion that finds its ultimate meaning in Christ's suffering, death and resurrection cannot afford to ignore total pain, a manifestation of meaning for those in its midst. Such a communion can speak to this despair, recognizing its source but ultimately, and sensitively, proclaiming hope in Christ (2 Cor. 4.16–18).

Recognizing and yet carefully resituating despair is one perspective that the communion of saints can offer. Coming from a holistic understanding of the human person, similar to that exemplified in total pain, it nonetheless carries this understanding beyond death, thus beyond the vain worldly aims highlighted above, and beyond that which might form part of the cause of the existential dread in the first place. Simply to tell someone suffering from great pain that 'all will be all right in the end', or even that there is hope beyond death, may be more than that individual can cope with, and it may certainly have quite the opposite effect to that desired. The challenge for our communication of doctrine is to find how to proclaim this truth in ways (perhaps spoken but as much lived out, as Saunders did in her explicitly Christian but non-proselytizing hospices) that recognize both realities, experience and doctrine, and find ways to enable the two to co-exist and converse.

It is reasonable to assume that 'until all of us come to the unity of the faith and the knowledge of the Son of God, to maturity, to the measure of the full stature of Christ' (Eph. 4.13), the communion as a whole at least (and possibly those individuals within it post death) continues to grow in holiness. The Orthodox Church particularly emphasizes this ongoing growth in holiness,[10] which could be described as an ever-increasing fellowship, one with the other and with Christ himself (the unity of which Ephesians speaks). The refusal to accept that death is the end of this growth in holiness speaks to the redeemability of even the most dire and desperate situations, including those encountered in total pain. For some, this release may come while still alive on earth; for others, it may be after death. Yet fundamental to this is the assertion that such growth continues, and this speaks particularly to the fear of loss.

Being alone is the opposite of the belief in communion. Fellowship – perfection and unity – is the ultimate end of the human person-in-communion. 'Death has no more dominion ... for as in Adam all die: even so in Christ shall all be made alive', as the Easter Anthems proclaim.[11] Being made alive – the *vivens homo* – is growing into the fellowship that unity with Christ promises. As the ancient Latin hymn for Masses of the dead proclaims, 'May the martyrs receive you at your arrival and lead you to the holy city Jerusalem.'[12] Here, then, in liturgical form is the promise of communion: at death, our orientation changes, but not our place in communion. We may fear losing our place as it is now, but this doctrine declares that we are never outside the communion with the saints alongside us.

This speaks also to our feeling safe, accompanied and listened to in communion. The communion of saints as a reality tells us that even when we truly do feel despairing and alone, the greater reality is that we remain in fellowship with God and fellow saints. In Joshua Hordern's account, which we referred to on pp. 36–7, he speaks of the communion of saints, where he makes mention of how there 'can be a meeting of affective insight without bodily encounter', where one can 'learn from a saint long past of how the hope of reaching the homeland, of entering into rest, contextuali[zes] the suffering of life's journey' despite a lack of 'bodily proximity'.[13] A saint is, according to the doctrine of the communion, not 'long past' but rather in some way present. The 'therapeutic encounters' (Hordern) then increase, not only in number but in form. Saints are not simply historical accounts – although they offer historical examples for the contemporary Christian – they are also travelling companions alongside the sufferer. The saints may even be considered the 'elders of the church', whose prayers for healing are encouraged (James 5.14).

This confidence in the saints offers a significantly expanded understanding of Christian healing, beyond the narrow confines of 'miracle cures' and the proselytizing that Saunders sought to avoid in her own explicitly Christian foundation. A foundation that is embedded in the theology of the communion situates healing within a wider narrative that by its nature is missional, one that is confident in the prayers of the saints and that intentionally welcomes the sick into community as equal members. Patients retain their dignity as saints that bless and are blessed; suffering is not sought but is held as the property of the community rather than the patient alone. The patient becomes person once again, and in doing so may be able to process and even shed some of the social, psychological and spiritual aspects of total pain that were otherwise overwhelming. This intentional recognition of the shared nature of the Christian journey may also avoid emotional exhaustion in carers, which may have similar aetiology to total pain itself.[14]

Individuals may find comfort in a recognition that, moving from a theology that condemns despair, at least some experience of total pain might even be the most appropriate outcome given particular circumstances (although that doesn't let the wider Christian community off the hook for addressing those circumstances in whatever positive way they can do). This is a complex and challenging area, yet it must be possible that, for some, total pain is inevitable, whether by natural temperament, environment or a combination. This is not the same as accepting that total pain *in general* is something that Christian society should accept as fact, and it should not lead to any lessening of efforts to combat societal evils such as loneliness and poor social conditions that might increase the likelihood of any individual developing total pain. But given our fallen world, and the reality of a particular place and time featuring in an individual's narrative, it may be unavoidable for that individual. In such a case, the community may take on some of the responsibility of bearing the pain – and if not the pain, then the hope that they might wish the individual to experience.

Being held in communion

The person in total pain may look to the saints to hold their hope – to feel when they themselves are unable to feel, and to some extent to inhabit the constancy of hope that they are simply unable to live at that moment in time. The communion is an extended family, living and departed, which carries the burdens in the Spirit (the Comforter) – but also the hidden joys, loves, hopes and dreams – of those who at that moment need a helping hand. Within this family are guides and confidantes, good friends and those whose friendship is known only through their being part of the communion that carries the burden of a friend of the head. Knowing each other to know Christ, and knowing Christ to know each other, are the ultimate dynamics at the heart of the communion. It is through this dynamic that we know the saints to be guides and confidantes, advocates and witnesses for God and for us – saints that help us on our route to holiness, however hopeless it might seem.

One member may be 'in despair' for a time, but the communion is nonetheless present, offering vicarious support; sometimes bearing burdens, sometimes offering encouragement and correction, the latter being more palatable because of its intentional situatedness within the community of faith (2 Tim.

2.24–26). For Milbank, 'a faithful truth-telling friendship' is at the heart of the mission of the church, which expresses 'the character of God as hospitable and embracing of strangers'.[15] Part of that truth is that even 'total pain', despite the despair, will end, however impossible that might feel to the sufferer at the time. Part of the bearing witness to that truth is simply being alongside and explicitly recognizing the innate dignity and *imago* of the sufferer.

Scott Bader-Saye suggests that 'the body has a unity that does not destroy difference ... [it] can only function based on the differences of the members'. He describes this (referencing Paul's imagery of the body of Christ) in a meditation on hospitality in the context of 'a culture of fear', suggesting that 'difference can be held together in a unity of purpose, in an eternal dance of love in which we are all invited to participate'.[16] While it would be absurd to wish for despair on our neighbour, nonetheless it appears that the biblical witness recognizes the importance of levels of individuality within the communal, and this individuality will include differences of temperament and situation. A communion that includes those with total pain most certainly needs this kind of intentional approach to hospitality. However uncomfortable, each person's contribution to the whole is essential.

Andrew Howell and Denise Larsen describe vicarious hope as a primarily self-transcendent project, in which a focus is placed on the needs of others, and 'egoism has been overshadowed by altruism'.[17] They suggest that this 'will be associated with improved levels of psychological functioning as it reflects an adaptive acceptance of one's situation', which enables 'ongoing *generativity*'.[18] This is, perhaps, the natural endpoint of any secular therapeutic approach to loss of hope, relating back to the biopsychosocial model and the 'contained' total pain. It is, in essence, a tacit acceptance that human existence is primarily individual, yet when individual notions of success or life-fulfilment fail, then an intentional increase in 'altruism' is required in order to overcome this 'egoism'. Yet such altruism appears primarily related only to those in close relation to the sufferer and is employed only when 'the person is "fearing the worst but yearning for better"'.[19] The 'better' on offer is a displacement of concern, not an addressing of the concern. While such a therapeutic approach may be effective in increasing 'psychological functioning', it does nothing to address the metaphysical questions of meaning that are rightly being asked in this scenario. Sheol ultimately remains the endpoint – separation and loss are simply obscured.

Fellowship and companionship

This is the key difference that holding the concept of total pain up against the communion of saints makes. The human person is entire and cannot be deconstructed, and the human person finds their meaning and ultimate destiny in fellowship with God and others, living and departed. This fellowship is tangible and lived, not simply abstract, and this fellowship has the potential to make a significant difference in the life of the Christian. It is a fellowship that fundamentally rejects loss and embraces and embodies resurrection, and it is a fellowship that can corporately hold on to faith, hope and love, however weakly it is held by the individual. This life *in via* with the saints ultimately points towards the life in glory, not only because of the promise of the resurrection but because the union with God and perfection in him is so clearly foreshadowed in the communion of the saints, in which are so clearly seen the virtues of faith, hope and love.

At heart, this is a 'theology *in via*' – 'an attentive openness of the whole self' – a facet of the *theologie totale* of Sarah Coakley,[20] in which contemplation meets a 'counterpoint of philosophy [and] science'. This *in via* aspect is in concordance with the concept of journeying discussed throughout these chapters, leading to a theology that remains contingent, responsive, and that is ultimately furthered in fellowship, fellowship that might be best described as companionship along the way. A commitment to this kind of dialogue is surely to be welcomed by Christians and carers alike.

John Thomson considers the church in the context of Milbank's ideas of 'radical friendship', noting 'this glimpse [of

God's future] is a hopeful sign', which Milbank describes as 'the continuing event of charity'.[21] This appears an apposite description of what the doctrine of the communion of saints offers in the context of total pain. Again, Thomson sees as central to Milbank's project the 'recovering [of] ... Aquinas's view of the church as a community of charity and friendship', a description that encapsulates much of what has been discussed here. Augustine and Aquinas see 'the church as a social and transmortal community of pilgrims whose charity and friendship are ... derived from ... the social holiness integral to the Christian story'.[22] It is such a community that Christians profess in the communion of saints in the creeds of the church, and it is such a community that best lays the foundation for loving fellowship with those most in need.

Notes

1 David Cheetham, *Creation & Religious Pluralism: A Christian Theology* (Oxford: Oxford University Press, 2020), p. 94.

2 For a discussion, see Geoff MacDonald and Lauri A. Jensen-Campbell, eds, *Social Pain: Neuropsychological and Health Implications of Loss and Exclusion* (Washington DC: American Psychological Association, 2011).

3 John Milbank, *Theology and Social Theory: Beyond Secular Reason* (London: Wiley, 2008), p. 417.

4 International Reformed–Anglican Dialogue, The Hiroshima Report *Koinonia: God's Gift and Calling* (2020), p. 29.

5 Bryn Davis, *Caring for People in Pain* (London: Routledge, 2000), eBook, section 11.

6 As developed in his work: René Girard, *The Scapegoat* (Baltimore: Johns Hopkins University Press, 1986).

7 The Hiroshima Report, pp. 29–30.

8 Sarah Grogan, *Body Image: Understanding Body Dissatisfaction in Men, Women and Children*, 3rd edn (Abingdon: Routledge, 2017), p. 11.

9 Stephen Ellingson, 'New research on megachurches', in Bryan S. Turner, ed., *The New Blackwell Companion to the Sociology of Religion* (Chichester: Wiley, 2016), p. 254.

10 Bryn Geffert and Theofanis G. Stavrou, *Eastern Orthodox Christianity: The Essential Texts* (New Haven: Yale University Press, 2016), p. 192.

11 Church of England, 'The Easter Anthems', www.churchofeng
land.org/prayer-and-worship/worship-texts-and-resources/common-
worship/common-material/canticles-main-12 (accessed 12.06.2021).

12 Michael Patella OSB, *Word and Image: The Hermeneutics of the Saint John's Bible* (Collegeville: Liturgical Press, 2005), p. 91.

13 Joshua Hordern, *Compassion in Healthcare: Pilgrimage, Practice, and Civic Life* (Oxford: Oxford University Press, 2020), p. 93.

14 Wilmar Schaufeli and Dirk Enzmann, *The Burnout Companion to Study and Practice: A Critical Analysis* (London: Taylor & Francis, 1998), p. 33.

15 John B. Thomson, *Sharing Friendship: Exploring Anglican Character, Vocation, Witness and Mission* (Abingdon: Routledge, 2016), p. 68.

16 Scott Bader-Saye, *Following Jesus in a Culture of Fear: Christian Practice of Everyday Life* (Grand Rapids: Brazos Press, 2007), p. 109.

17 Andrew J. Howell and Denise J. Larsen, *Understanding Other-Oriented Hope: An Integral Concept within Hope Studies* (Cham: Springer, 2015), p. 60.

18 Howell and Larsen, *Understanding Other-Oriented Hope*, p. 61.

19 Howell and Larsen, *Understanding Other-Oriented Hope*, p. 60, quoting Richard S. Lazarus, *Emotion and Adaptation* (New York: Oxford University Press, 1991), p. 282.

20 Sarah Coakley, *God, Sexuality and the Self: An Essay 'On the Trinity'* (Cambridge: Cambridge University Press, 2013), p. 88.

21 Thomson, *Sharing Friendship*, p. 71.

22 Thomson, *Sharing Friendship*, p. 68.

7

Pain in communion

We have examined the impact that attentiveness to the doctrine of the communion of saints might have on us as we seek to come alongside and fully embrace those who suffer 'total pain'. At this stage, we might also seek to ask what 'total pain' might say to our understanding of Christian doctrine. Despite Saunders' – and our – refusal to immediately dismiss those suffering as somehow deficient in membership of the Christian community (and in the case of this book, of the communion more widely), there remains a sense of challenge in recognizing that there might be those whose experience of life no longer offers them a sense of hope. We have thought about this in the context of the community holding hope – of the communion bearing witness to this hope – yet we must ask what the impact might be on our self-understanding as a church if we take this despair as a *given* rather than attempt to ignore it. To an extent, our recognizing of the existence of 'total pain' requires us to ask what this ultimately reveals about Christian life in its totality.

Aetiology of total pain

As we saw in Chapter 2, it is futile and ultimately unhelpful for us to focus on attempting a simplistic understanding of the 'why' of the presence of evil. 'Total pain', in that it entails despair and a lack of hope in Christ, appears to be something similarly challenging to understand fully. Let us not be misunderstood – it is certainly possible to understand elements of the 'how' of pain, and address these. These might include societal factors, biological factors and so on, all of which come with a sense of responsibility for Christians to address. Yet this is not the same as understanding the 'why', and this 'why' impacts our self-understanding.

Ultimately, we recognize that by its very existence 'total pain' must challenge our ability (albeit theoretical) to abolish all human suffering through human means. This may not come as a surprise from a Christian perspective, although in wider society this truth might be less readily received. Those suffering from total pain may indeed be helped by the holistic model of care that Saunders conceived of, and it may be the case that some might be drawn out of this existential dread towards a way of facing death that loses some of the power of despair of total pain. Our next chapter considers some ways that we might address this from a pastoral perspective. Yet unless we conceive of 'total pain' in entirely reductive terms – as something to which God is incidental and which, were we to embrace and implement 'best practice', we might be able to completely avoid – we must also recognize that it poses a challenge to our self-understanding. It is by no means clear that any such best practice exists.

We might argue, then, that total pain – far from being an unfortunate and yet ultimately calculable and thus solvable side-effect of the dying process – is actually a normal part of the human experience. If we do so, then we might connect it with other moments of despair in the human condition, not only those associated with dying but those that, for example, might be experienced by others in response to the horrendous evils spoken of by Marilyn McCord Adams, which 'can reasonably bring participants to the point of despair'.[1] To call something normal is not to call it good, yet to recognize it as part of the human experience is to accept that it may have a rightful place within human life. We can address this in two ways. Questions might arise as to how God might permit this to be the case, where hope is seen as a fundamental virtue of Christian living. Or questions might focus, instead, on how we best respond to this as a fact of life.

The former set of questions once again returns us to conversations about the meaning of evil, or at least the meaning of those things that appear, objectively, not to be 'good'. It is hard to see immediately what innate benefits there might be in 'total pain' (most certainly to the individual suffering it), and hence we might be led to explain it by way of the Fall, something that has entered into human existence not through God's good plan but by disobedience. Total pain might be described as part of the wider category of 'suffering' (although it rightly includes both suffering *and* a loss of hope), and much has been written about the association between suffering and the Fall, although this is by no means an open-and-closed discussion.[2] It is not at all clear that such reasoning gives us much in the way of understanding in this particular instance; total pain's great central element, despair, is a lack or absence of hope *despite* and in the face of the saving power of the cross and resurrection of Christ. In a sense, it is a post-resurrection lack of 'good', something whose roots might be partially explained by Fall theology, and yet something that surely has a more complicated theological ecology.

Yet it does not, ultimately, appear to be a fruitful enterprise to focus on asking about the aetiology of suffering from a theological perspective. For the theologian, it is more interesting and useful, perhaps, to ask what this suffering *and* lack of hope can tell us about our doctrines and how it might refine them. In a sense, the question becomes not so much 'Why is suffering permitted?', but, 'How do our doctrines stand up in the light of the reality of suffering and the lack of hope that it entails?' It is here that we might ask: how does 'total pain' engage with the communion of saints? Is there coherence in such a conversation between them? If so, what might that coherence be, and what are its implications?

Spiritual implications of communion

This brings us back to the theme of our Introduction. Christian doctrine in itself is of little worth if it does not have any impact on how we live as Christian disciples. In Chapter 2, we considered what the role of the community might be in responding to evil, and stated:

To respond in solidarity (either as agents of the mercy of God, or responding in a 'humane' or indeed more fully human way in terms of sociality, as we shall see) is to actively participate in God's response to evil, and to participate is to realize our humanity more fully.

We must now recognize that these implications are significantly strengthened in form if we are to hold them within the light of our doctrine of the communion of saints. If we are to recognize the insights of the last chapter, we cannot do this in isolation; they must reframe both our practice and our self-understanding. This means asking what historical and current attitudes, behaviours and teachings of the church might need to be tempered, refined or re-engaged with by a lived belief in the communion of saints, and how this might enable the church better to respond to the challenges posed by the existence of total pain. Our response to despair, for example, cannot be one in which we simply deny its existence; we must grapple with it as a reality.

The communion of saints demands not only that we recognize the existence of total pain but also that we see it as somehow 'other'. Our belief in the ultimate interconnectedness of humanity across time and space does not leave us with any option but to recognize the ultimate interconnectedness even of those things that we might find uncomfortable. Our conception of the individual-in-communion means that while total pain might be suffered by one particular individual, nonetheless it affects the body of the communion more widely. It becomes more than a simple process of suffering of 'the other' that we can shut away; it becomes something that affects each of us through our connection in communion. Not only will this have pastoral implications, but theological as well. We are faced with the reality that total pain is not only a mystery for the individuals suffering it but a wider mystery that speaks to the entirety of the communion. Total pain becomes part of our sociality and our self-definition. We are a communion that can suffer total pain – albeit in part.

This has an impact on us, too, as a church. We must ultimately include it within any self-definition. The participatory nature of the communion, both with one another and ultimately with the Godhead, necessitates that we no longer see total pain as a problem to solve for others, but rather find it as a 'social' entity. We move beyond sympathy, therefore, to a widened concept of empathy that recognizes not only our responsibility to come alongside others in total pain but also to find ways to speak of total pain as a social reality that impacts each of us. It moves us beyond lukewarm expressions of sympathy towards rediscovering the ultimate situating of compassion within companionship. Solidarity is no longer something we choose, but something that is of our human nature, as humans within communion. Our choice becomes whether we recognize the reality of our interconnectedness, rather than whether that interconnectedness exists.

In short, we *are* in communion, and total pain *is* a lived reality within that communion. Our responding in a 'more fully human way' is to respond as co-participants in something that spans time and space and that makes demands on us – demands of sociality that in themselves help us to find our definition as truly human and 'realize our humanity more fully'. This sociality is a work of the Holy Spirit. Here we recognize the Holy Spirit as comforter, as the God that confirms and strengthens our sociality. Our commitment to communion-participation in those things we call 'good' and those things we call 'bad' that are experienced by others is how we become more fully human. Becoming more human is, therefore, being filled more with the Holy Spirit, and in so doing we conform ourselves more to Christ and more fully display the *imago Dei*.

It is through communion that we most fully realize our own individuality, an individuality that ultimately cannot exist apart from this communion. Such an individuality-in-communion is therefore an individuality of love, a love that reflects the New Commandment, and the communion is empowered by the Holy Spirit that enables us to love as Christ loved us:

> I give you a new commandment, that you love one another. Just as I have loved you, you also should love one another. By this everyone will know that you are my disciples, if you have love for one another. (John 13.34)

Here, then, we meet again the theological virtues and can see how even where one of these appears absent – where hope is replaced by despair – the communion of saints offers us a way of refusing this as the last word, instead helping us to find ways to hold vicariously that hope in faith and love (reflecting, perhaps, the theme of 1 Corinthians 13). Our solidarity becomes clear: our love for each other here is strong as death, but also strong as despair; our communion-in-love ultimately triumphs over the loss of hope that might affect the individual member and might appear to threaten us through our interrelatedness. Our communion becomes the ultimate definition of our lives together, and in doing so presents an unsurmountable challenge to fear and loss:

'Death has been swallowed up in victory.'
'Where, O death, is your victory?
    Where, O death, is your sting?'
(1 Cor. 15.54–55)

Practical implications of communion

This recasting of life together in spiritual terms must not, of course, remain distinct from its practical and pastoral implications. However, it is key for us to recognize that these practical and pastoral implications are as a result of these spiritual realities rather than separate from them; it is not that we do good things for our neighbour merely because we feel we ought, but because this is ultimately at the heart of becoming more human. This will inevitably make us address the question of the role of the church as part of the communion of saints, and the effects of the spiritual reality outlined above on the church as an institution.

We have previously raised the question about the boundaries of the communion of saints, whether it might include the whole of humanity (or, in some way, the whole created order). For now we must recognize the importance of the place of the church – however constituted, but certainly including its institutional form – in any self-understanding that springs from a commitment to this doctrine. This is challenging, not least because of the different emphases placed and perspectives held by different churches in their relationship with this particular doctrine (for example, the role of veneration, prayer for the dead, and so on). Nonetheless, we must ask what the implications might be for the church in at least general terms.

We might start by considering biblical injunctions on this topic. Philippians 2 is a key text in this context, as there is an explicit link made between the actions of the church and the 'mind ... that was in Christ Jesus'. Paul exhorts them:

> If, then, there is any encouragement in Christ, any consolation from love, any sharing in the Spirit, any compassion and sympathy, make my joy complete: be of the same mind, having the same love, being in full accord and of one mind. Do nothing from selfish ambition or conceit, but in humility regard others as better than yourselves. Let each of you look not to your own interests, but to the interests of others. (vv. 1–4)

Similarly in Romans 12–15, Paul makes reference to the church's members as part of one body, and hence with interlinking responsibilities:

> For as in one body we have many members, and not all the members have the same function, so we, who are many, are one body in Christ, and individually we are members one of another. We have gifts that differ according to the grace given to us: prophecy, in proportion to faith; ministry, in ministering; the teacher, in teaching; the exhorter, in exhortation; the giver, in generosity; the leader, in diligence; the compassionate, in cheerfulness.
>
> Let love be genuine; hate what is evil; hold fast to what is good; love one another with mutual affection; outdo one another in showing honour. Do not lag in zeal, be ardent in spirit, serve the Lord. Rejoice in hope, be patient in suffering, persevere in prayer. Contribute to the needs of the saints; extend hospitality to strangers.
>
> Bless those who persecute you; bless and do not curse them. Rejoice with those who rejoice, weep with those who weep.

Made explicit here is the importance of weeping with those who weep, and the source of that command being that 'we, who are many, are one body in Christ, and individually we are members one of another'. Writing to two different Christian communities, Paul makes it clear that it is part of the self-understanding and spiritual self-definition of the communities themselves that they do these things. Hebrews 10.24–25, too, makes clear the link between 'love and good deeds' and 'meet[ing] together', highlighting the role of the Christian community in these works of love:

> And let us consider how to provoke one another to love and good deeds, not neglecting to meet together, as is the habit of some, but encouraging one another, and all the more as you see the Day approaching.

Similarly, we find these links made explicit in the Westminster Confession:

> All saints, that are united to Jesus Christ their Head, by his Spirit, and by faith, have fellowship with him in his graces, sufferings, death, resurrection, and glory: and, being united to one another in love, they have communion in each other's gifts and graces, and are obliged to the performance of such duties, public and private, as do conduce to their mutual good, both in the inward and outward man.
>
> Saints by profession are bound to maintain an holy fellowship and communion in the worship of God, and in performing such other spiritual services as tend to their mutual edification; as also in relieving each other in outward things, according to their several abilities and necessities. Which communion, as God offereth opportunity, is to be extended unto all those who, in every place, call upon the name of the Lord Jesus.[3]

In each of these texts, there is no place to make a neat but ultimately false distinction between 'spiritual services' and 'relieving each other in outward things'. While the Westminster Confession makes reference to these as categories, they are clearly interwoven in the life of the church. We see a similar perspective elucidated in the formulation of the Five Marks of Mission as discussed in Chapter 1. Hence the church's response to total pain must include both of these categories and yet also see them as ultimately indistinguishable. 'The worship of God', we might say, includes the 'outward things' that those in communion do one for the other.

Aquinas's sermon on the Apostles' Creed gives an account with a somewhat different emphasis, that of sacramentality:

> Just as in a physical body the operation of one member redounds to the good of the whole body, so it works in a spiritual body, that is to say, in the church. Since all the faithful are one body, the good of one is communicated to another. Paul writes:
>
> '[Thus, we who are many are one body in Christ,] individuals, yet members one of the other' (Rom. 12.5). Thus, among other matters which should be believed that the apostles handed down, there remains the communion of goods in the church. This [doctrine] is called 'the communion of saints.'
>
> Among all the other members of the Church, however, the principal member is Christ, for he is the head of the church: '[And he put down everything under his feet, and] he put himself as head over the whole church, which is his body, [the fullness of him who fulfills everything in everyone]' (Eph. 1.22–23). Therefore the good of Christ is communicated to all Christians, as the wisdom of the Head is communicated to all the members. This communion comes about through the sacraments of the church, in which the strength of the passion of Christ for conferring grace and for forgiving sins operates.[4]

This is a helpful reminder that while the church's worship may include 'outward things', that is, pastoral and practical elements, it is also the place where Christians situate their sacramentality. This sacramentality must not be forgotten in any discussion of the church, but neither must it lead to a 'spiritualizing' of the practical engagement that Paul calls us to in the light of the doctrine of the communion of saints. This remains a tension across all parts of the church's life but, for those in 'total pain', their membership of the communion (if we are to take the most reductive form) must surely be assured through the very sacramentality of baptism. A serious and engaged response to 'total pain' – both institutionally and through its members – is not only good but essential for the church to pursue and provide, not least because of the incorporation of those in 'total pain' through baptism in the communion. In a sense, it is owed to them by virtue of this incorporation.

We might take issue with Aquinas's somewhat unidirectional understanding of sacramentality (through the church to the church), but nonetheless his reference to this sacramentality is helpful because it reminds us that the church – as, we might say, a visible expression of communion – is called to 'confer' grace in the sacraments to 'all members'. We might see this as reaching beyond the sacraments themselves to a wider understanding of sacramentality – a pointing towards 'the eschatological future that the Church looks [to] in hope and anticipation'.[5] A commitment to sacramentality might be described as a pursuing of and participation in a narrative of grace that infuses each act that the church undertakes. It is in the proclamation and living out of such a narrative that the church – as institution and as its members – might best engage with the reality of 'total pain'.

The communion as challenge

At this point, we might address a challenging question. We have spoken much about a recognition of total pain and its impact on the wider body of the church, but it remains the case that a lack of hope continues to be jarring to much in Christian theology. We might, therefore, ask ourselves whether there is a place for challenge as part of the Christian – and the church's – response to total pain. Is there, in other words, a place for prophetic challenge when encountering people in total pain?

Surely the answer to this question is found in how that challenge might be presented. The entire thrust of our reflections to date would suggest that a proselytizing and declarative challenge would be both inappropriate and ultimately fruitless.

As Saunders recognized, even within explicitly Christian organizations like her hospice, it was not appropriate or helpful to proselytize. Yet there may well be a place for the church to engage with this topic in what might be described as a prophylactic way, addressing issues of death and dying with frankness and openness as part of wider mission, something that does not appear to be done with confidence (as we discussed in Chapter 1). A focus on a convincing and integrated theology of hope in death would be no small contribution to equipping people with the tools to engage with periods of existential dread, even if it might not remove them entirely. Our absence from this space is lamentable and must most certainly be reversed if we are to hope to use the proclamation of the gospel of hope in a way that can be heard and received at a time when this might be possible.

Hope, too, might not always be best expressed in the spoken word, but in the wider existential reality of the church and of those living intentionally in the light of communion. The church is itself a sign of this hope, its sacramentality speaking to this ultimate 'eschatological Christian hope [which] is inseparable from an incarnational involvement in the struggle of living and contemporary humanity'.[6] This hope is, by nature, future-looking and is quite separate from optimism. For those facing death, optimism may indeed be quite perverse, yet part of the role of the church must surely be to point to glimpses of hope and hold them as true, even if they cannot be believed by the sufferer of total pain. Hope might, then, be prophetically engendered by the church.

The hospice movement, and the underlying philosophical and theological thinking of Cicely Saunders, might provide the impetus and imagination for the church to move forward in this area and identify ways of being not only a place of challenge but also a place of comfort and understanding, which themselves embody such hope. Saunders 'opened up a practical, personal, political and philosophical space for engaging with the care of the dying, and with death itself', combining 'warmth and solicitude', and where she 'listened carefully to patients' stories', concerned 'both *with* persons and *as* persons'. David Clark tells us:

This new approach embraced rather than retreated from the intersubjective experience of care at the end of life, recognizing that *everyone* involved is touched in some way. It privileged the otherwise abandoned and stigmatized dying individual by insisting that 'you matter because you are you'.[7]

This narrative approach is something that the church might adopt not only in its engagement with total pain but in its self-understanding more generally. Hospice life is, perhaps, a glimpse of what life lived out in communion might seek to be – a place tinged with hope despite appearances, built in love, sustained by prayer and committed to listening. 'You matter because you are you,' recalls the *imago Dei,* and we might seek to add to it by suggesting, 'You matter because you are you to God, and because you are you to me.' The communion of saints tells us that this relationship matters – relationship to God and to each other. It is to practical ways of envisioning this relationship that we now turn.

Notes

1 Marilyn McCord Adams, *Horrendous Evils and the Goodness of God* (Ithaca: Cornell, 1999), p. 203.

2 An interesting conversation on this topic in the light of the theory of evolution can be found in James K. A. Smith and William T. Cavanaugh, eds, *Evolution and the Fall* (Grand Rapids: Eerdmans, 2017).

3 Bob Burridge, 'Survey Studies in Reformed Theology: Ecclesiology – Lesson 2 – Of the Communion of Saints', *Genevan Institute for Reformed Studies* (2002, 2011), http://genevaninstitute.org/syllabus/unit-six-ecclesiology/lesson-2-of-the-communion-of-saints/ (accessed 01.12.2022).

4 Nicholas Ayo C. S. C., ed., *The Sermon-Conferences of St. Thomas Aquinas on the Apostles' Creed* (Eugene: Wipf and Stock, 1988), p. 135.

5 Geoffrey Rowell, 'The significance of sacramentality', in Geoffrey Rowell and Christine Hall, eds, *The Gestures of God: Explorations in Sacramentality* (London: Continuum, 2004). p. 5.

6 Naomi Burton Stone and Patrick Hart, eds, *Thomas Merton: Love and Living* (San Diego: Harcourt Brace Jovanovich, 2002), p. 156.

7 David Clark, 'Works of Love: Cicely Saunders and the Hospice Movement', *Open Democracy* (14 July 2015), www.opendemocracy.net/en/transformation/works-of-love-cicely-saunders-and-hospice-movement/ (05.03.2022).

8

Insights for ministry and pastoral practice

So far in this book we have asked questions about what a reorientation and focus on our doctrine, and a holding up of this doctrine in the light of human experience, and vice versa, might tell us about our fundamental self-understanding as people, as Christians and as Christians-in-community. In the previous chapter we looked at this question from the point of view of the church, and in doing so saw the fundamental interweaving of the church's inner nature and its sacramental calling. In this chapter, we will seek to address how this calling might be borne out in the pastoral practice of the church and its ministers, lay and ordained.

It is important, of course, to recognize that what we now know about total pain may not be the last word – indeed, it is unlikely to be so. The underlying perspective of the whole human person, entire and not compartmentalized, is a key insight that has developed out of a Christian milieu, and is one that speaks to the 'dignity and rights' that accompany discussions of the human person in the secular world.[1] Yet the application of any such perspective must be accompanied by a serious investigation of and interface with research in the natural and social sciences. As we have previously intimated, theology done in a vacuum is of limited use – science and theology in serious dialogue reveal theology that is 'respectful of the past but open to future developments, cautious in discernment but also courageous in the face of truth', which is far more likely to be both defensible and importantly provide better pastoral practice in the ministry and mission of the church.[2]

The particular conception of total pain that we have met and expanded has wider application across the other sciences and indeed within medicine. As described earlier, the resistance to this concept in pain medicine has led to a far more functional and compartmentalized, treatment-oriented yet anthropologically weak understanding of pain through the biopsychosocial model. By engaging in serious dialogue, theologians and pastors have much to offer to the medical field – to all fields in which there is the possibility of engaging anthropological models. Limited progress in this area is a sad reflection on a lack of confidence and a reluctance to progress this dialogue in a way that respects and understands the scientific method.

The church as pastor

Ministry and pastoral practice remain far too often seen as the preserve of the clergy, at least in the popular mind, and the church as an institution is on occasion an unpopular entity. However, to take the communion of saints seriously, there must be some connection with the church as it is – we have seen the communion described as the 'nourishment' of the church in an earlier chapter. Moving away from a church of the exceptional or of the 'professional Christian' appears to offer a more fruitful and coherent pastoral approach than to think of the priest dispensing the benefits of the church like a gift to those in total pain (albeit while at the same time not ignoring the sacramental). As we have seen, *koinonia* is a gift to us all without exception. Our pastoral engagement must surely be one that recognizes the precedence of this gift and then works out our response to it as something that speaks deeply to us about the meaning and function of the church.

Pastoral practice that builds on our refined anthropology is ultimately one of person-in-community and not necessarily focused on the individual pastoral 'practitioner'. The priest or minister stands as symbol of the wider church; it is in the wider church (and beyond) that the doctrine finds its truest fulfilment, and it is therefore from this wider church and communion that the most effective pastoral responses are likely to come. A church seeking to meet those in total pain might best meet them as co-members of the communion, affirming their place in the crowd of witnesses rather than offering easy answers or simplistic 'relief'. That is not to suggest there is nothing to do in pastoral terms – this is not to enforce a false binary – but rather to recognize that the 'coming alongsideness' of Christian ministry, a 'coming alongsideness' that is clearly situated in belief but that does not insist on proselytizing, may sometimes not only be good but the best response we might make.

Here we return to the theme of 'accompaniment' and to the remembrance that the Christian's ultimate fellowship is with Christ. In Bonhoeffer's terms, 'the church is where the presence of Christ exists as community', and we participate in rather than create such community, which is of God by essence.[3] Maury Jackson links this understanding to Milbank's suggestion that 'the life of the saints is inherently social, because it is the opposite of a life of sin, which is the life of self-love'.[4] This offers a reinterpretation of the sin of despair of which Aquinas speaks; ultimately, the community can act as at least partial remedy to any such sin. Developing Bonhoeffer's idea beyond the church on earth to a full conception of the communion of saints simply widens both the Christ-centredness and the reach of the pastoral life. As we have discussed, the 'sin' of despair may be a demonstration of corporate or structural, rather than individual, sin, and thus not only might the church's coming alongside those in total pain offer relief, but it might also have metaphysical implications.

Total pain appears to relate ultimately to fear, loss and 'aloneness'. It is incumbent upon churches to become communities in which this fear can be enunciated, but also communities where the communion is lived so tangibly that those who might begin to feel this way are buffered by the knowledge that they remain a valued part of the communion. Until churches can say this for their own members, it is challenging to see how they might enable this for others beyond their doors.

In practice, this will mean intentional opportunities to live out the concepts of reciprocity and relationship, of those being blessed also being those who bless. Much of this already forms much of the basis of church activity, yet there remain concerns that churches do not reach out to many on the margins, for example disabled people. Indeed, 'disabled people cite the attitudes, environment and barriers to participation as being the most disabling factors in their lives', and the Church of England recognizes that 'the Church has often made [and continues to make] mistakes in this area and overlooked the calling and gifts of disabled people'.[5] It is only through being intentionally welcoming, but also affirming the 'dignity of each [person] as a human being, precious to God and man', that individual churches can truly model the communion of which they are a part.[6]

As we have seen, those in total pain can fulfil the role of scapegoat and thus find themselves excluded and ignored by otherwise 'happy' church communities. Of course, we are not called to happiness per se; we are called to 'joy', certainly, but a joy grounded in the hope of the resurrection rather than in a worldly, and false, optimism. Yet it is not only physical exclusion from the church that might be present, although this is certainly a potential risk, with those in hospital, hospice or dying at home being seen as an 'optional extra' for already overstretched pastoral visitors, including clergy who might otherwise bring the sacrament. Exclusion can also take the form of theological visibility. Churches that preach a theology but will not or cannot engage with issues of despair, hopelessness and human fear will ultimately fail large numbers of their members.

True hospitality genuinely affirms people as part of co-humanity.[7] This requires a casting off of preconceptions, prejudices and the temptation to create the communion in our own image, and can only be aided by deliberately reorienting our fellowship with each other as fundamentally reliant upon fellowship with Christ. It is through this fellowship that the 'aloneness' that defines total pain can best be avoided. Specific practices can come from this intentional embodying of communion – among them intercession, the willingness of Christians to listen alongside others, and an increased focus on chaplaincy among those at risk of feeling most alone. Seeking out the 'company and sympathy of friends' is recommended by Aquinas, not least because being able to 'confide in others, and receive their support' leads to a lessening of the weight of sorrow; 'When our friends console us, we see that we are loved by them, and that is a source of joy.' Such friends may not have a theodicy but they nonetheless lighten the burden.[8] Some practices will start at the point of total pain, but it may be that the most effective ways to combat it are found in a healthy community that meets and lives in communion well before any individual member encounters despair.

Friendship with the saints through the ages

Another practical outworking of this fellowship might be an encouragement to make friends with particular saints – such as recommended by Anselm – through learning about their lives and their faith journeys, and most particularly by considering them as a group of friends from whom we, who remain on earth, have much to learn. There are numerous examples of those in the communion who have faced death, despair and annihilation, among them the martyrs, fathers and mothers of the early church. Hordern notes that 'to know something of the loss of a parent through Augustine's eyes and in personal experience may cast surprising light on the nature of compassion'.[9] This is one example whereby the experiences of the saints might prove to be living examples alongside us, assisting, cajoling, educating and encouraging the saints on earth.

Other examples might be St John of the Cross and Teresa of Avila, who 'give us such interesting clues about the relation of physical pain and suffering to spiritual pain and suffering and thus about that mysterious ... gap between physical manifestations and subjective response'.[10] The experiences of the saints might prove to be living examples alongside us, assisting, cajoling, educating and encouraging the saints on earth. Coakley argues that these saints tell us that 'a lifetime's commitment to prayer ... is more likely to *intensify* spiritual "pain" than to alleviate it ... but that this purgative pain may eventually give way ... to the qualitatively higher state of transformed "union"'.[11] She notes the 'communal significance' of this transformation because of its reordering of the narrative about (in this case) St Teresa in the eyes of the community, pain being seen as 'a curative part of the divine purpose for the soul's good', 'a sign of the soul's straying from the path', or 'as a serendipitous event that can nonetheless be woven purgatively into God's plan'.[12] It is clear that there is 'no one theory' of pain in the history of Christianity and hence among the saints of the communion, yet it is also clear that saints – including those who have faced despair – offer a number of different perspectives that may prove edifying (or quite the opposite) to those in total pain.[13] To make the acquaintance of these thinkers is surely a gift of the Christian church.

The multifarious understanding of and engagement with pain within the communion is doubtless inevitable, given its holding of meaning and the search for meaning within it discussed earlier. It is also a corrective to easy answers, and highlights once again that the true gift is one of accompaniment and not theodicy or trite attempted relief. A desire instead for empathy may well enable effective compassionate relationships that are 'marked by engagement in the life-course, patience, curiosity, humility, a qualified commitment to the value of healthcare, and perseverance in companionship'.[14] At times, this compassion may require us, following Augustine, to 'grieve not just over the sins of [ourselves and our] fellow human beings but over their misery as well: the misery of poverty, the misery ensuing on the death of friends, the misery of intractable pain'.[15] While Laurence Kirmayer suggests that we may have an 'inability to tolerate vicarious pain and accept our own powerlessness to alleviate the suffering of others',[16] it may be a gift of the communion to express compassion through solidarity and an owning of that pain as a form of communal meaning. This may be how the communion best shares the pain of its members, recognizing both our limited ability to truly empathize and our declaration that this pain is communally our own.

It is not only through conversation with the saints that we

might find them to be friends. While different theologies may clash over the validity of the belief in the power of invocation or in the mechanism of the interaction of the saints in glory with us who remain on earth, nonetheless one thing we must surely do is proclaim and live out a faith and a theology that demonstrates our belief in there being some significance to our membership of a body that passes through time and space. For more catholic-minded Christians, it is certainly the case that any professed belief in the efficacy of the prayers of the saints must be visible and concordant with elements of pastoral practice. The key point here is not so much what our specific belief is in this realm (although we must do the theological work that enables us to defend our position); the priority must be in communicating in word and deed that we are part of a communion of saints that 'refers to those who live in Christ who "died for all", so that what each one does or suffers in and for Christ bears fruit for all'.[17] This requires a commitment to communality within the church, and a recognition that this communality does not end with the church on earth. In doing so, we ultimately resituate pain as a social entity.

The role of the liturgy

A way of holding this pain and marking it as communal may be through liturgy in gathered community. Already liturgies exist that mark a commonality of purpose, solidarity and grief. The naming of the deceased during the Eucharistic Prayer of the Roman Catholic Church points towards the communion, and it may be that there are forms of service or elements that can be incorporated into current acts of worship that achieve a similar function. Once again, this increases the visibility of the communal, showing defiance to loss and the raw individuation so feared by those in total pain. It may not be possible to make the unbearable bearable, or to reduce the feeling of loss, but it is nonetheless important to find practical ways to hold, and to demonstrate the holding of, hope. That pain (and its association yet not total elision with suffering[18]) is to some extent culturally and socially mediated has been covered extensively in this book. That the communion of saints, with all its theological implications for loss and despair, is made present and visible in culture must surely be part of the role of the church militant. Liturgy, as the 'source and summit of our Christian life' whose stuff is 'enormous meaning' and the 'Church's prayer',[19] must surely form a key part in any response to the meaning found in pain and loss suffered in a community, often described through narrative.[20]

This might take a variety of forms. In the first instance, we must make sure that the language we use in the liturgy reflects our underlying beliefs. An example might be drawing attention to our asking the intercession of the saints (for example, the Hail Mary), reciting the Te Deum or praying the end of the Preface in the Eucharistic Prayer, as we described earlier. This is from the *Common Worship* liturgy of the Church of England:

> Therefore with angels and archangels,
> and with all the company of heaven,
> we proclaim your great and glorious name,
> for ever praising you and *saying*:

> **Holy, holy, holy Lord,**
> **God of power and might,**
> **heaven and earth are full of your glory.**
> **Hosanna in the highest.**
> **Blessed is he who comes in the name of the Lord.**
> **Hosanna in the highest.**[21]

Yet we must also be clear that simply mentioning the doctrine is not ultimately enough. (Here we might note with interest that the use of the Nicene Creed, frequently that proclaimed during eucharistic worship, rather than the Apostles' Creed, which we might find during non-eucharistic daily worship, does not explicitly mention the communion of saints.) Proper catechism and teaching must take place to make these links explicit, speaking not only of the communion in the abstract but linking it to the reality of human lives as they are lived, and the shared nature of the good and the bad within them.

A particular example of where attention is drawn to the communion, and to the hope that it engenders, is a funeral. We began this book by suggesting that there is much to do in this area, and from our reflection throughout we must now return to this topic. The Christian faith neither obviates the real, felt, human sadness associated with death, nor does it accept a narrative that claims that death is the end. Funerals are a key place where this reality might be proclaimed, once again in word and deed. We do not seek to be prescriptive here in terms of liturgy, vestments and other content; instead, we call for a renewed focus on ensuring that what we do and say in our liturgical practice is aligned with our underlying beliefs. The 'Choristers' Prayer' puts this simply:

Bless, O Lord, us Thy servants who minister in Thy temple.
Grant that what we sing with our lips we may believe in
    our hearts,
and what we believe in our hearts we may show forth in
    our lives.
Through Jesus Christ our Lord. Amen.[22]

This is the guiding principle that must influence us as we live out the Christian faith. This may, at times, prove difficult. It may be that we need to exert significant pastoral accommodation to ensure that particular readings or family requests are not dismissed out of hand, even if they appear to clash with our theological outlook. Yet, as funerals become more and more a choice industry, we must be clear about what it is that a Christian funeral entails, and what is the impetus for our offering such an office. Our funeral liturgy must not be something ad hoc or unrelated to our wider theological and liturgical landscape; it must, like the Book of Common Prayer liturgy referenced in the Introduction, be part of the total fabric of our lives together as Christians. If we are shying away from funeral ministry, we must ask ourselves why this is the case, and address this in the light of the reality of the communion of saints. To refuse to do so is to harm both those attending funerals and those facing death. Our lives as Christians are interdependent, and proper attention paid to the communion of saints makes this explicit. This is both a mission imperative and a mission opportunity.

Theologies of trauma and lament

Part of our enunciating this vision will also necessitate us pointing to the witness of the scriptures. There are biblical texts that might speak particularly well to people in total pain, among them Job and Ecclesiastes. Theologies of trauma and lament are also commonly found in the academic literature,[23] but it may be that these have not yet been effectively distilled into church practice.[24] Churches that retain the liturgical year may find this process easier; the desolation of Holy Saturday or the embraced grief of commemorations of the faithful departed may enable such a theological understanding to be more easily woven into the church's liturgical life. As noted previously, the church's deficit in its pastoral response to suicide has not been fully resolved, and it appears necessary that the church seriously revise its practice, liturgical and otherwise, in the light of a real and present communion.

For example, it may not be that 'man rejects God's mercy, and by presumption, His justice' when falling into despair.[25] It may simply be that the reality of the world in which that person lives leads them to find no tangible hope, a result not of rejecting God but of circumstances conspiring against the individual with no relief. We are told by Aquinas to 'despair of no man in this life, considering God's omnipotence and mercy'.[26] Perhaps it is our role as the church to attempt to relieve, and at least pray, rather than condemn. More thought needs to be given to the practical out-workings of this in our church communities.

One way to address this potential issue would be to make narrative theology more of a focus in the way we engage with people suffering with despair, and those who end their own lives in suicide. There remains a deep chasm of loss in the lives of those who lose family or friends to suicide, and this is not addressed pastorally by simplistic and reductive comment on suicide as 'the unforgivable sin that separates Christians from

God'.[27] Not only is this a position that ultimately leads to increased stigma that hinders 'help, support, and care', but it also shows a fundamental misunderstanding of the aetiology and impact of serious mental health conditions. Clergy and churches hold a significant potential role in being places where despair and suicidal thinking might be engaged with, discussed and met pastorally in a space that feels safe enough to take the existential pressure that such conversations might need. Such spaces might be kind and focus on listening, understanding the narrative of suicidal thinking in a way that does not reduce the human being to this one emotion or emotional state but rather views them as the fully integrated person that Saunders' perspective envisioned. A focus on this integrated narrative takes away the temptation to reduce individuals to the set of actions we see directly in front of us. This is useful not only in the engagement with those suffering total pain but is far more widely applicable.

Listening and kindness might be the best ways for churches to engage more generally with questions of human suffering, death, despair, suicidal thinking, and other related issues such as bereavement, trauma, lament and loneliness. This is not the same as giving up the ground on which these things might be discussed or adopting a supposedly neutral viewpoint that gives the impression that the church has nothing to say on these matters. However, it is to recognize that despair and these other emotional states are real experiences that have an impact on those within and without the church, and which cannot be simply and easily waved away or ignored. The first step in resolving – or seeking to resolve – others' pain and suffering is to listen to what they say about it.

Our language in this area matters. A particular example might be how we engage with issues of assisted dying. The Church of England's most recent position paper on assisted dying states the following: 'The wishes and aspirations of individuals are important, but it is not possible to view these in isolation from the effects that they might have on other individuals and on society in general.'[28] While we might see something of the narrative of communion that we have discussed within these words, what is ostensibly missing from this paper is any direct reference to the lived experience of those seeking assisted dying, those in despair, or any reference at all to total pain. The paper refers to hospice care, stating: 'In particular, the excellent care pioneered by the hospice movement has demonstrated that holistic, palliative care which treats every individual with respect and dignity and is a viable, life-affirming alternative to assisted suicide.' This may well be true, but questions remain unanswered about what to do when this 'alternative' is not seen as 'viable' and 'life-affirming', and whether a refusal to listen to people's narratives is truly treating them with 'respect and dignity'. The position paper further states that 'while assisted suicide is contrary to the principles outlined above, other end of life decisions ought to be respected', and yet does so without any apparent engagement whatsoever with the narratives of those who might seek such an outcome, however much the church might – both historically and currently – disagree with the reasoning that leads to this outcome or indeed the outcome itself. The purpose of this commentary is not to suggest the church changes its teaching; it is, instead, a call for the church to change how it engages with such issues. Doing so might also have the effect of our being listened to ourselves more by those with whom we disagree.

Advocacy

Finally, as part of its witness to the communion in charity and solidarity, the church also has a responsibility to challenge the unjust structures of society that might form contributory factors in the development of total pain. It may be that, for some, total pain is inevitable, yet as noted it is often found to be a mixture of the temperamental and the environmental. Poor housing, limited social support, inability to pay medical bills, and many other elements, may contribute to the fear and loss (and untreated physical or mental pain) that ultimately builds up total pain. This aim is fundamental to the mission of the church and, as we have described, is mentioned explicitly in the Five Marks of Mission of the Anglican Communion.[29] Once again, however, it is key that the theological underpinning of these mission imperatives is made clear; the communion of saints is a communion of solidarity with our neighbours under Christ, and to this end this mark is not optional. To claim to hold another's pain as one's own while doing nothing to relieve the suffering in any concrete or practical way is at best a mis-representation of one's own position.

Total pain reminds Christians that we remain in an 'already but not yet' kingdom, in which the reign of Christ has begun but in which our fallenness continues to affect our relationships and our experience of the world. A recognition and accept-ance that despair continues to afflict those in our communities, and in our communion, is not heretical but rather should call us to become a church in which these evils of suffering are, where possible, ameliorated, avoided and alleviated. It is not our place as a church to simply pretend they do not exist. The church must become a place of hospitality to the afflicted, one that stands with them in solidarity. Indeed, the church forms part of the communion through the ages whose members stand alongside each other, oriented to Christ. Our own journey as a church, as a ministerial and pastoral entity with solidarity and accompaniment at its heart, must be to better model that reality.

Notes

1 Samuel Moyn, *Christian Human Rights* (Philadelphia: University of Penn Press, 2015), pp. 99–100.

2 Giuseppe Tanzella-Nitti, 'Natural Sciences, in the Work of Theo-logians', *INTERS.org* (2008), https://inters.org/natural-sciences (accessed 08.03.2022).

3 Maury Jackson, 'Ecclesiology and Theodicy: Bonhoeffer's *Sanc-torum Communio* as Response to Human Suffering', *Testamentum Imperium* 5 (2016), pp. 1–26; p. 17.

4 Jackson, 'Ecclesiology and Theodicy', p. 21.

5 Church of England, 'Welcoming disabled people', www.churchof england.org/resources/welcoming-disabled-people (accessed 12.06.2021).

6 Allen Verhey, *The Christian Art of Dying: Learning from Jesus* (Grand Rapids: Eerdmans, 2011), p. 61.

7 Joseph L. Mangina, *Karl Barth: Theologian of Christian Witness* (Louisville: Westminster John Knox Press, 2004), p. 96.

8 Andrew Davison, 'Thomas Aquinas, lifestyle coach – sound advice from a thirteenth-century saint', *Church Times* (26 March 2021), www.churchtimes.co.uk/articles/2021/26-march/features/features/thomas-aquinas-lifestyle-coach (accessed 12.06.2021).

9 Joshua Hordern, *Compassion in Healthcare* (Oxford: Oxford University Press, 2020), p. 93.

10 Sarah Coakley, 'Palliative or intensification? Pain and Christian contemplation in the spirituality of the sixteenth-century Caermelites', in Sarah Coakley and Kay Kaufman Shelemay, eds, *Pain and Its Transformations: The Interface of Biology and Culture* (Cambridge, MA: Harvard University Press, 2007), p. 79.

11 Coakley, 'Palliative or intensification?', p. 79.

12 Coakley, 'Palliative or intensification?', p. 80.

13 Coakley, 'Palliative or intensification?'. p. 90.

14 Hordern, *Compassion in Healthcare*, p. 255.

15 Nicholas Wolterstoff, 'The place of pain in the space of good and evil', in Coakley and Kaufman Shelemay, eds, *Pain and Its Transformations*, p. 413.

16 Laurence J. Kirmayer, 'On the cultural mediation of pain', in Coakley and Kaufman Shelemay, eds, *Pain and Its Transformations*, p. 381.

17 The Vatican, *Catechism of the Catholic Church* (London: Bloomsbury Academic, 2002), para. 961.

18 Smadar Bustan, 'Diagnosing human suffering and pain: Integrating phenomenology in science and medicine', in Simon van Rysewyk, ed., *Meanings of Pain – Volume 2: Common Types of Pain and Langauge* (Cham: Springer Nature Switzerland, 2019), pp. 46–50.

19 Corinna Laughlin, *The Liturgy: The Source and Summit of Our Christian Life* (Chicago: Archdiocese of Chicago Liturgy Training Publications, 2018), p. 12.

20 Frank C. Senn, *Introduction to Christian Liturgy* (Minneapolis: Fortress Press, 2012), p. 10.

21 Church of England, 'Holy Communion Service', www.churchofengland.org/prayer-and-worship/worship-texts-and-resources/common-worship/holy-communion-service#mm7c5 (accessed 02.12.2022).

22 RSCM America, 'What We Do', www.rscmamerica.org/what-we-do (accessed 02.12.2022).

23 For example, see Walter Brueggemann, *The Psalms and the Life of Faith* (Minneapolis: Fortress Press, 1995), and Serene Jones, *Trauma + Grace: Theology in a Ruptured World* (Louisville: Westminster John Knox Press, 2009).

24 For discussion on this topic, see Megan Warner, Christopher Southgate, Carla A. Grosch-Miller and Hilary Ison, eds, *Tragedies and Christian Congregations: The Practical Theology of Trauma* (Abingdon: Routledge, 2019).

25 Thomas Aquinas, *Summa Theologiae* (Second Part of the Second Part, Question 14: Article 2, Objection 1), translated at New Advent, www.newadvent.org/summa/3014.htm (accessed 12.06.2021).

26 Thomas Aquinas, *Summa Theologiae* (Second Part of the Second Part, Question 14: Article 3, Reply to Objection 1), translated at New Advent, www.newadvent.org/summa/3014.htm (accessed 12.06.2021).

27 John Potter, 'Is Suicide the Unforgivable Sin? Understanding Suicide, Stigma, and Salvation through Two Christian Perspectives', *Religions* 12(11) (2021) p. 987.

28 Brendan McCarthy, 'Why the Church of England Supports the Current Law on Assisted Suicide', www.churchofengland.org/sites/default/files/2017–11/Assisted%20Suicide%20and%20the%20Church%20of%20England.pdf (accessed 01.12.2022).

29 Anglican Communion, 'Marks of Mission', www.anglicancommunion.org/mission/marks-of-mission.aspx (accessed 30.11.2022).

9

Conclusion

Throughout the preceding pages, we have undertaken an interrogation of a key Christian doctrine and asked whether paying further attention to its underlying narrative about humanity might aid us in engaging with parts of the human story that are far too often ignored or held at arm's length. Saunders' concept of 'total pain' speaks both experientially and theologically in this conversation, as a way of addressing the human person holistically and without casting judgement on the individual. The doctrine of the communion of saints and the reality of 'total pain' have much to say to one another, not only in a theological milieu but in terms of our pastoral and ministerial practice as a church and as Christians. There is here both coherence and helpful tension. Through this, the church might find a way to engage more fully, generously and helpfully with those in despair, while at the same time gain more in the way of self-understanding. It is a potentially very fruitful exercise and speaks to the importance of constantly refining and interrogating our doctrines in the light of human experience – and vice versa. Saunders' willingness to think theologically in the first place aids us in this pursuit, yet the church too has a responsibility to refuse to shy away from serious conversation in this area. There is much work to be done.

Baptism and incorporation in the communion

A final point remains unresolved, and has been alluded to on a number of occasions throughout our exploration: what are the bounds of this communion? In the first instance, it is worth stating that the bounds are not something for humankind to determine – this is properly the domain of God. Yet we are certain to wonder what the bounds might be. Would the communion include all the living baptized, and exclude those who are not? How about after death? These are not new questions, and different denominations have struggled with these questions of Christian belonging (and in some cases attempted to resolve them, albeit in a contingent way).

There is no intention to come to any kind of conclusion, contingent or otherwise, on this matter here, and it is important to recognize that while the communion of saints is (or should be) a key part of the great majority of theological traditions, nonetheless individual interpretations will vary and the approach to these issues will not be uniform. This will relate not least to interpretations of the Fall and of salvation through Christ, and hence individual and corporate contributions to both of these. The existence of the communion of saints does, however, offer a corrective when the communal (and the importance of the communal) is laid aside. Whatever our conception of these particular doctrines, we must always ultimately see ourselves as part of something – the communion of saints.

It is therefore not contradictory potentially to hold a loose definition of entry into the communion while at the same time placing a greater emphasis on and in baptism than we might currently do. The Church of England's baptism liturgy describes it in the following terms in the Pastoral Introduction:

> Baptism marks the beginning of a journey with God which continues for the rest of our lives, the first step in response to God's love. For all involved, particularly the candidates but also parents, godparents and sponsors, it is a joyful moment when we rejoice in what God has done for us in Christ, making serious promises and declaring the faith. The wider community of the local church and friends welcome the new Christian, promising support and prayer for the future. Hearing and doing these things provides an opportunity to remember our own baptism and reflect on the progress made on that journey, which is now to be shared with this new member of the Church.[1]

We might ask whether these definitions should be expanded to take account of the reality of the communion of saints. It is important to make clear that 'the church' is a temporal manifestation of the communion, yet we surely lose something from our self-understanding – a self-understanding that we then communicate with the catechumens – if we do not make explicit the continuity with the communion of saints more generally. The 'communion of saints' is mentioned only during the Apostles' Creed in both baptism and confirmation as found in *Common Worship* and the Book of Common Prayer. It is important that it is mentioned here, but this does appear of limited use given our exploration so far. Baptism, as a rite of initiation, is a significant teaching opportunity and is surely a place where we might commit ourselves publicly to this key tenet of the Christian faith.

We might then strengthen the link between baptism and the reception of Holy Communion, speaking of *koinonia* in a more unified and coherent way that makes direct links between its different aspects within the theology we proclaim. It is logically consistent that we ask for initiation before the reception of communion, yet by speaking of this in terms of *koinonia* we might find a way to communicate that does not carry with it some of the exclusiveness that has been claimed in some parts of the Anglican Church.[2] Once again, it is in honing in on our doctrine and assessing its implications that we might better adapt and refine our practice.

The narrative of communion

A key finding in this book has been the importance of narrative – and of the particular narrative that is followed – in the life of the Christian. We have seen a belief in the communion of saints to be an expression of a Trinitarian and pneumatological reality, an expression of the human person in community, as interdependent and reliant on the lifeblood of the Holy Spirit. This is a communion in and of love, which is rooted in faith and steeped in future hope. It is the way of life of the Christian and an outpouring of the grace of God. It is the truth in which we find meaning and which sustains the life of the people of God.

Companionship in communion is one of its gifts to its members, and that companionship encompasses compassion, empathy and friendship. The etymology of the word points helpfully towards the eucharistic, sacramental life that all are called to share. While those in total pain face fear and loss, this sacramental living and fellowship proclaims that, despite everything, this experience is not the final word. The church on earth and all that it corporately experiences is – by nature – contingent, and yet this contingency remains embedded in eschatological hope of the kingdom to come and resurrection life beyond the grave. It is from these truths that total pain might be addressed, with proclamation and with way of life.

This way of life of human beings, on a journey towards ultimate fulfilment, is reflected in the narrative form of scripture and in the theology of participation in the life of God. Narrative is not incidental to life in communion, but is central to it. This narrative can yield meaning, and being open to the narrative of others can enrich our own Christian journey. Recognizing the realities of human life but not being beholden to all the claims they might make on us is one of the key implications and gifts of living in communion. Our story is part of the whole but is not complete without its interaction with other stories, and theirs with ours.

'The dying have much to teach us'

We began our exploration by stating this very clear fact – one that has surely been shown to be true throughout this book. Yet perhaps we might expand it too – the dying *and* the dead have much to teach us, and much more than simply teach. Our relationship with one another as Christians does not end at death, just as the relationship of Christ with us and the relationship at the heart of the Holy Trinity did not end with Christ's own death on the cross. We live this mystery, a mystery of relationship, sociality and communion.

Our life is lived for others, never solely for ourselves. The perfect human life of Jesus Christ was likewise oriented outwards, lived for the glory of God and for the salvation of all humankind. The church has much still to say to the world, despite everything we might hear and despite all our divisions and disagreement – perhaps because of them, too. The communion of saints exists – and it matters. It is now for us more fully to open ourselves up to participate in the creative and redemptive will of God, and in so doing to reveal the relationship that sits at the heart of everything it is to be human.

Notes

1 Church of England, 'Baptism and Confirmation', www.church ofengland.org/prayer-and-worship/worship-texts-and-resources/ common-worship/christian-initiation/baptism-and#mm017 (accessed 01.12.2022).

2 Bosco Peters, 'Baptism – Communion – which order?', *Liturgy* (2012), https://liturgy.co.nz/baptism-communion-2 (accessed 05.11.2022).

Bibliography

Adams, M. McCord, *Horrendous Evils and the Goodness of God* (Ithaca: Cornell, 1999).

al'Absi, M. and Flaten, M. A., eds, *The Neuroscience of Pain, Stress, and Emotion* (London: Elsevier, 2016).

Anderson, A., *An Introduction to Pentecostalism: Global Charismatic Christianity* (Cambridge: Canterbury University Press, 2004).

Anglican Communion, 'Marks of Mission' www.anglicancommunion. org/mission/marks-of-mission.aspx (accessed 30.11.2022).

Anglican Communion News Service, 'Anglican provinces declare "impaired" or "broken" relationship with ECUSA' (9 December 2003), www.anglicannews.org/news/2003/12/anglican-provinces-declare-impaired-or-broken-relationship-with-ecusa.aspx (accessed 10.11.2022).

Anselm, *The Prayers and Meditations of St Anselm with the Proslogion*, trans. B. Ward (London: Penguin, 2006).

Aquinas, T., *Summa Theologiae* translated at New Advent, www.newadvent.org/summa/3014.htm and www.newadvent.org/summa/3020.htm (accessed 12.06.2021).

Ayo, N., ed., *The Sermon-Conferences of St. Thomas Aquinas on the Apostles' Creed* (Eugene: Wipf and Stock, 1988).

Bader-Saye, S., *Following Jesus in a Culture of Fear: Christian Practice of Everyday Life* (Grand Rapids: Brazos Press, 2007).

Barth, K., *The Faith of the Church: A Commentary on the Apostles' Creed According to Calvin's Catechism* (Eugene: Wipf and Stock, 2006).

Barth, K., *Prayer*, trans. S. F. Terrien (Philadelphia: Westminster Press, 1952).

Baum, G., *Essays in Critical Theology* (London: Sheed and Ward, 1994).

Beauchamp, T. L. and Childress, J. F., *Principles of Biomedical Ethics* (Oxford: Oxford University Press, 2001).

Bell, C., *Queer Holiness* (London: Darton, Longman and Todd, 2022).

Bergmann, S., ed., *Eschatology as Imagining the End: Faith between Hope and Despair* (Abingdon: Routledge, 2018).

Bezzant, R. S., *Jonathan Edwards and the Church* (Oxford: Oxford University Press, 2014).

Bilateral Working Group of the German National Bishops' Conference and the Church Leadership of the United Evangelical Lutheran Church of Germany, *Communio Sanctorum: The Church as the Communion of Saints*, trans. M. W. Jeske, M. Root and D. R. Smith (Collegeville: Liturgical Press, 2004).

Bloesch, D. G., *The Last Things: Resurrection, Judgment, Glory* (Downers Grove: InterVarsity Press, 2004).

Booth, P. and Tingle, E., eds, *A Companion to Death, Burial, and Remembrance in Late Medieval and Early Modern Europe, c.1300–1700* (Leiden: Brill, 2020).

Bountra, C. et al., eds, *Pain: Current Understanding, Emerging Therapies, and Novel Approaches to Drug Discovery* (New York: Marcel Dekker, Inc., 2003).

Brueggemann, W., *The Psalms and the Life of Faith* (Minneapolis: Fortress Press, 1995).

Burrell, D. B., *Deconstructing Theodicy: Why Job has Nothing to Say to the Puzzle of Suffering* (Grand Rapids: Brazos, 2008).

Burridge, B., 'Survey Studies in Reformed Theology: Ecclesiology – Lesson 2 – Of the Communion of Saints', *Genevan Institute for Reformed Studies* (2002, 2011), http://genevaninstitute.org/syllabus/unit-six-ecclesiology/lesson-2-of-the-communion-of-saints/ (accessed 01.12.2022).

Burton Stone, N. and Hart, P., eds, *Thomas Merton: Love and Living* (San Diego: Harcourt Brace Jovanovich, 2002).

Catholic Academy of Liturgy, *A Commentary on the Order of Mass of The Roman Missal* (Collegeville: Liturgical Press, 2011).

Chamberlain, A., ed., *The Works of Jonathan Edwards, Volume 18, The 'Miscellanies'* (New Haven: Yale University Press, 2000).

Chapman, M., Clarke, S. and Percy, M., eds, *The Oxford Handbook of Anglican Studies* (Oxford: Oxford University Press, 2015).

Cheetham, D., *Creation & Religious Pluralism: A Christian Theology* (Oxford: Oxford University Press, 2020).

Church of England, 'At the Burial of the Dead', www.churchofengland.org/prayer-and-worship/worship-texts-and-resources/book-common-prayer/burial-dead (accessed 02.12.2022).

Church of England, 'Baptism and Confirmation', www.churchofengland.org/prayer-and-worship/worship-texts-and-resources/common-worship/christian-initiation/baptism-and#mm017 (accessed 01.12.2022).

Church of England, 'Funeral', www.churchofengland.org/prayer-and-worship/worship-texts-and-resources/common-worship/death-and-dying/funeral#mm121 (accessed 15.11.2022).

Church of England, 'Holy Communion Service', www.churchofengland.org/prayer-and-worship/worship-texts-and-resources/common-worship/holy-communion-service#mm7c5 (accessed 02.12.2022).

Church of England, 'Learning to Pray', www.churchofengland.org/prayer-and-worship/learning-pray (accessed 02.12.2022).

Church of England, 'The Easter Anthems', www.churchofengland.org/prayer-and-worship/worship-texts-and-resources/common-worship/common-material/canticles-main-12 [accessed 12.06.2022).

Church of England, 'The Lord's Supper or Holy Communion', www.churchofengland.org/prayer-and-worship/worship-texts-and-resources/book-common-prayer/lords-supper-or-holy-communion (accessed 12.06.2021).

Church of England, 'The Order for Morning Prayer', www.churchofengland.org/prayer-and-worship/worship-texts-and-resources/book-common-prayer/order-morning-prayer (accessed 12.06.2021).

Church of England, 'Welcoming Disabled People', www.churchofengland.org/resources/welcoming-disabled-people (accessed 12.06.2021).

Clark, D., *Cicely Saunders: A Life and Legacy* (Oxford: Oxford University Press, 2018).

Clark, D., *To Comfort Always: A History of Palliative Medicine since the Nineteenth Century* (Oxford: Oxford University Press, 2016).

Clark, D., '"Total pain", Disciplinary Power and the Body in the Work of Cicely Saunders, 1958–1967', *Social Science and Medicine* 49 (1999), pp. 727–36.

Clark, D., '"Total pain": The Work of Cicely Saunders and the Maturing of a Concept', *End of Life Studies* (University of Glasgow, academic blogs), 25 September 2014, http://endoflifestudies.academicblogs.co.uk/total-pain-the-work-of-cicely-saunders-and-the-maturing-of-a-concept/#_edn4 (accessed 12.06.2021).

Classen, A. and Sandidge, M., eds, *Friendship in the Middle Ages and Early Modern Age* (Berlin: Walter de Gruyter, 2010).

Coakley, S., *God, Sexuality, and the Self: An Essay 'On the Trinity'* (Cambridge: Cambridge University Press, 2013).

Coakley, S. and Kaufman Shelemay, K., eds, *Pain and Its Transformations: The Interface of Biology and Culture* (Cambridge, MA: Harvard University Press, 2007).

Cook, C. H. and Hamley, I., *The Bible and Mental Health* (London: SCM Press, 2020).

Cooke, B. and Macy, G., *Christian Symbol and Ritual: An Introduction* (Oxford: Oxford University Press, 2005).

Danaher, W. J., Jr, *The Trinitarian Ethics of Jonathan Edwards* (Louisville: Westminster John Knox Press, 2004).

Davis, B., *Caring for People in Pain* (London: Routledge, 2000).

Davis, E. and Hays, R. B., eds, *The Art of Reading Scripture* (Grand Rapids: Eerdmans, 2003).

Davison, A., 'Thomas Aquinas, lifestyle coach – sound advice from a thirteenth-century saint', *Church Times* (26 March 2021), www.

churchtimes.co.uk/articles/2021/26-march/features/features/thomas-aquinas-lifestyle-coach (accessed 12.06.2021).

Dehaene, S., *The Cognitive Neuroscience of Consciousness* (Cambridge: MIT Press, 2001).

DeLorenzo, L. J., 'Belief in the Communion of Saints Isn't Optional', *Church Life Journal* (2 November 2017), https://churchlifejournal. nd.edu/articles/belief-in-the-communion-of-saints-isnt-optional/ (accessed 12.06.2021).

Dick, K. L. and Buttaro, T. M., eds, *Case Studies in Geriatric Primary Care & Multimorbidity Management* (St Louis: Elsevier Inc., 2020).

Dillenberger, J., ed., *Martin Luther: Selections from His Writings* (New York: Knopf Doubleday Publishing Group, 2011).

Diocese of Shrewsbury, 'The Communion of Saints', www.diocese ofshrewsbury.org/faith-and-life/creed/the-communion-of-saints (accessed 20.03.2022).

Ebert, M. H. and Kerns, R. D., *Behavioural and Psychopharmacologic Pain Management* (Cambridge: Cambridge University Press, 2011).

Ehrman, B. D., *Heaven and Hell: A History of the Afterlife* (New York: Simon and Schuster, 2020).

Eilers, K. and Strobel, K., eds, *Sanctified by Grace: A Theology of the Christian Life* (London: Bloomsbury, 2014).

Ekstrom, L. W., *God, Suffering, and the Value of Free Will* (Oxford: Oxford University Press, 2021).

Emergy, P.-Y., *The Communion of Saints*, trans. D. J. Watson and M. Watson (London: Faith Press, 1966).

Encyclopaedia Britannica, 'Te Deum laudamus', www.britannica.com/ topic/Te-Deum-laudamus (accessed 12.06.2021).

Engel, G. L., 'The Need for a New Medical Model: A Challenge for Biomedicine', *Science* 196(4286) (8 April 1977), pp. 129–36.

Flint, T. and Rea, M., eds, *The Oxford Handbook of Philosophical Theology* (Oxford: Oxford University Press, 2009).

Frankl, V. E., *Man's Search for Meaning* (London: Rider, 2013).

Geffert, B. and Stavrou, T. G., *Eastern Orthodox Christianity: The Essential Texts* (New Haven: Yale University Press, 2016).

Girard, R., *The Scapegoat* (Baltimore: Johns Hopkins University Press, 1986).

Goulding, G., 'Reformation and Recusants: Christian Unity and the Communion of Saints', *Pro Ecclesia: A Journal of Catholic and Evangelical Theology* 26(1) (2017), pp. 49–55.

Grenz, S. J., *Theology for the Community of God* (Grand Rapids: Eerdmans, 1994).

Grogan, S., *Body Image: Understanding Body Dissatisfaction in Men, Women and Children*, 3rd edn (Abingdon: Routledge, 2017).

Hahn, S., *Angels and Saints: A Biblical Guide to Friendship with God's Holy Ones* (New York: Image, 2014).

Harvard Health Publishing: Harvard Medical School, 'What causes depression?', 24 June 2019, www.health.harvard.edu/mind-and-mood/what-causes-depression (accessed 12.06.2021).

Herbermann, C. G. et al., eds, *The Catholic Encyclopedia, Volume 8* (New York: Robert Appleton Company, 1910).

Hodge, C., *A Commentary on the Epistle to the Ephesians* (New York: Robert Carter & Brothers, 1856).

Holley, D., *Meaning and Mystery: What it Means to Believe in God* (Oxford: Blackwell, 2010).

Hooten, W. M., 'Chronic Pain and Mental Health Disorders: Shared Neural Mechanisms, Epidemiology, and Treatment', *Mayo Clin Proc.* (2016 July; 91(7)) pp.955-70

Hordern, J., *Compassion in Healthcare: Pilgrimage, Practice, and Civic Life* (Oxford: Oxford University Press, 2020).

Howell, A. J. and Larsen, D. J., *Understanding Other-Oriented Hope: An Integral Concept within Hope Studies* (Cham: Springer, 2015).

Hummel, L. M. and Woloschak, G. E., *Chance, Necessity, Love: An Evolutionary Theory of Cancer* (Eugene: Cascade, 2017).

Hylands-White, N., et al., 'An Overview of Treatment Approaches for Chronic Pain Management', *Rheumatology International* 37 (2017), pp. 29–42.

International Reformed–Anglican Dialogue, The Hiroshima Report, *Koinonia: God's Gift and Calling* (2020).

Jackson, M., 'Ecclesiology and Theodicy: Bonhoeffer's *Sanctorum Communio* as Response to Human Suffering', *Testamentum Imperium* 5 (2016), pp. 1–26.

Jones, S., *Trauma + Grace: Theology in a Ruptured World* (Louisville: Westminster John Knox Press, 2009).

Kaba, R., and Sooriakumaran, P., 'The Evolution of the Doctor–Patient Relationship', *International Journal of Surgery* 5(1) (2007), pp. 57–65.

Kaltwasser, C., 'Karl Barth on What Makes us Human', *The Thread: Princeton Theological Seminary*, https://thethread.ptsem.edu/culture/karl-bath-on-what-makes-us-human (accessed 12.06.2021).

Kierkegaard, S., *The Sickness Unto Death: A Christian Psychological Exposition of Edification and Awakening by Anti-Climacus* (London: Penguin, 2004).

Kissane, D. W. et al., eds, *Handbook of Communication in Oncology and Palliative Care* (Oxford: Oxford University Press, 2010).

Kuyper, A., *The Work of the Holy Spirit*, trans. H. de Vries (New York: Cosimo, 2007).

Ladd, G. E., *A Theology of the New Testament*, rev. edn (Grand Rapids: Eerdmans, 1993).

Lampard, J., 'The Future of Christian Funerals', in The Methodist Church, *The Epworth Review*, www.methodist.org.uk/our-faith/life-and-faith/theology/the-epworth-review/ (accessed 02.12.2022).

Laughlin, C., *The Liturgy: The Source and Summit of Our Christian Life* (Chicago: Archdiocese of Chicago Liturgy Training Publications, 2018).

Lazarus, R. S., *Emotion and Adaptation* (New York: Oxford University Press, 1991).

MacDonald, G. and Jensen-Campbell, L. A., eds, *Social Pain: Neuropsychological and Health Implications of Loss and Exclusion* (Washington DC: American Psychological Association, 2011).

Mangina, J. L., *Karl Barth: Theologian of Christian Witness* (Louisville: Westminster John Knox Press, 2004).

Mazza, E., *The Celebration of the Eucharist: The Origin of the Rite and the Development of Its Interpretation*, trans. Matthew J. O'Connell (Collegeville: Liturgical Press, 1999).

McBrayer, J. and Howard-Snyder, D., eds, *The Blackwell Companion to the Problem of Evil* (Hoboken: Wiley-Blackwell, 2014).

McCarthy, B., 'Why the Church of England Supports the Current Law on Assisted Suicide', www.churchofengland.org/sites/default/files/2017-11/Assisted%20Suicide%20and%20the%20Church%20of%20England.pdf (accessed 01.12.2022).

McCarthy, G., *Introduction to Metaphysics* (Waltham Abbey: ED-Tech Press, 2018).

McClymond M. J. and McDermott, G. R., *The Theology of Jonathan Edwards* (New York: Oxford University Press, 2012).

Milbank, J., *Theology and Social Theory: Beyond Secular Reason* (London: Wiley, 2008).

Miller, M. R., 'Aquinas on the Passion of Despair', *New Blackfriars* 93(1046) (2011),pp. 387–96.

Millspaugh, D., 'Assessment and Response to Spiritual Pain: Part I', *Journal of Palliative Medicine* 8(5) (2005), pp. 919–923.

Mitchell, G., ed., *Palliative Care: A Patient-centred Approach* (Boca Raton: CRC Press, 2008).

Moore, R., ed., *Biobehavioural Approaches to Pain* (New York: Springer, 2009).

Moreland A. M. and Dumas, J. E., 'Categorical and Dimensional Approaches to the Measurement of Disruptive Behaviour in the Preschool Years: A meta-analysis', *Clinical Psychology Review* 28(6) (July 2008), pp. 1059–70.

Moyn, S., *Christian Human Rights* (Philadelphia: University of Penn Press, 2015).

National Institute for Health and Care Excellence, 'Chronic pain (primary and secondary) in over 16s: Assessment of all chronic pain and management of chronic primary pain: NICE guideline [NG193]', 7 April 2021, www.nice.org.uk/guidance/ng193/chapter/recommendations (accessed 04.01.2022).

Nohrnberg, J., 'Three Phases of Metaphor, and the Mythos of the

Christian Religion: Dante, Spenser, Milton', *Spenser Studies: A Renaissance Poetry Annual* (2018), vol. XXXI/XXXII, pp. 613–49.

Ortlund, G. R., *Anselm's Pursuit of Joy: A Commentary on the Proslogion* (Washington DC: The Catholic University of America, 2020).

Patella OSB, M., *Word and Image: The Hermeneutics of The Saint John's Bible* (Collegeville: Liturgical Press, 2005).

Pauw, A. P., '*The Supreme Harmony of All': The Trinitarian Theology of Jonathan Edwards* (Grand Rapids: Eerdsmans, 2002).

Pearson, L., ed., *Death and Dying: Current Issues in the Treatment of the Dying Person* (Cleveland: The Press of Case Western Reserve University, 1969).

Pelikan, J., *Credo: Historical and Theological Guide to Creeds and Confessions of Faith in the Christian Tradition* (New Haven: Yale University Press, 2005).

Peters, B., 'Baptism – Communion – which order?', *Liturgy* (2012), https://liturgy.co.nz/baptism-communion-2 (accessed 05.11.2022).

Pfund, R. and Fowler-Kerry, S., eds, *Perspectives on Palliative Care for Children and Young People: A Global Discourse* (Oxford: Radcliffe, 2010).

Potter, J., 'Is Suicide the Unforgivable Sin? Understanding Suicide, Stigma, and Salvation through Two Christian Perspectives', *Religions* 12(11) (2021) p. 987.

Rahner, K., *Theological Investigations: Volume 3*, trans. C. Ernst (Limerick: Mary Immaculate College, 2000).

Ramsey, H., 'Death Part 3: Our Attitude Towards Death', *New Blackfriars* 86(1004) (2005), pp. 418–24.

Ratzinger, J., *Meaning of Christian Brotherhood* (San Francisco: Ignatius, 2013).

Richardson, A. and Bowden, J., *A New Dictionary of Christian Theology* (London: SCM Press, 2002).

Rolheiser OMI, R., 'Despair as weakness rather than sin', *Angelus* (18 May 2017), https://angelusnews.com/voices/despair-as-weakness-rather-than-sin/ (accessed 12.06.2021).

Rowell, G. and Hall, C., eds, *The Gestures of God: Explorations in Sacramentality* (London: Continuum, 2004).

RSCM America, 'What we do', www.rscmamerica.org/what-we-do (accessed 02.12.2022).

Sanders, J., *Theology in the Flesh: How Embodiment and Culture Shape the Way We Think about Truth, Morality, and God* (Minneapolis: Fortress Press, 2016).

Saunders, C., 'Care of patients suffering from terminal illness at St Joseph's Hospice, Hackney, London', *Nursing Mirror* (14 February 1964), pp. vii–x.

Saunders, C., 'The Care of the Dying', *Guy's Hospital Gazette* 80 (1966), pp. 136–42.

Saunders, C., *Cicely Saunders: Selected Writings 1958–2004* (Oxford: Oxford University Press, 2006).

Saunders, C., 'The Evolution of Palliative Care', *Journal of the Royal Society of Medicine* 94(9) (2001), pp. 430–32.

Saunders, C., *The Management of Terminal Illness* (London: Hospital Medicine Publications Ltd, 1967).

Saunders, C., 'The Symptomatic Treatment of Incurable Malignant Disease', *Prescribers' Journal*, 4(4) (October 1964), pp. 68–73.

Schaufeli, W. and Enzmann, D., *The Burnout Companion to Study and Practice: A Critical Analysis* (London: Taylor & Francis Ltd., 1998).

Schwan, J. et al., 'Chronic Pain Management in the Elderly', *Anesthisology Clinics* 37(3) (2019), pp. 547–60.

Schwartz, J. M. and Begley, S., *The Mind and the Brain: Neuroplasticity and the Power of Mental Force* (New York: Harper Collins, 2002).

Senn, F.C., *Introduction to Christian Liturgy* (Minneapolis: Fortress Press, 2012).

Sheldrake, P., ed., *New SCM Dictionary of Christian Spirituality* (London: SCM Press, 2013).

Sheng, J. et al, 'The Link between Depression and Chronic Pain: Neural Mechanisms in the Brain, *Neural Plast* (2017, Article 9724371).

Shotter, E. F., ed., *Matters of Life and Death* (London: Darton, Longman and Todd, 1970.

Smith, J. K. A. and Cavanaugh, W. T., eds, *Evolution and the Fall* (Grand Rapids: Eerdmans, 2017).

Stahl, W., Campbell, R., Petry, Y., Diver, G., *Webs of Reality: Social Perspectives on Science and Religion* (Piscataway: Rutgers University Press, 2002).

Stark, R. and Bainbridge, W. S., *Religion, Deviance, and Social Control* (Abingdon: Routledge, 2013).

Swerdlow, M., ed., *The Therapy of Pain* (Lancaster: MTP Press, 1981).

Swinburne, R., *Providence and the Problem of Evil* (Oxford: Oxford University Press, 1998).

Tanzella-Nitti, G., 'Natural Sciences, in the Work of Theologians', *INTERS.org* (2008), https://inters.org/natural-sciences (accessed 08.03.2022).

Thomas, P., *Using the Book of Common Prayer* (London: Church House Publishing, 2012).

Thomson, J. B., *Sharing Friendship: Exploring Anglican Character, Vocation, Witness and Mission* (Abingdon: Routledge, 2016).

Turner, B. S., ed., *The New Blackwell Companion to the Sociology of Religion* (Chichester: Wiley, 2016).

van Rysewyk, S., ed., *Meanings of Pain – Volume 2: Common Types of Pain and Language* (Cham: Springer Nature Switzerland, 2019).

Vatican, *Catechism of the Catholic Church* (London: Bloomsbury Academic, 2002).

Verhey, A., *The Christian Art of Dying: Learning from Jesus* (Grand Rapids: Eerdmans, 2011).

Wald, F. S., ed., *Quest of the Spiritual Component of Care for the Terminally Ill: Proceedings of a Colloquium* (Yale: Yale University School of Nursing, 1986).

Walls, J., *Purgatory: The Logic of Total Transformation* (Oxford: Oxford University Press, 2012).

Warner, M. et al., eds, *Tragedies and Christian Congregations: The Practical Theology of Trauma* (Abingdon: Routledge, 2019).

Ware, K., *The Inner Kingdom* (Yonkers: St Vladimir's Seminary Press, 2020).

World Health Organization, *International Statistical Classification of Diseases and Related Health Problems 10th Revision (ICD-10) Version for 2010*, https://icd.who.int/browse10/2010/en#!/F32.3 (accessed 12.06.2021).

Zizioulas, J., *Being as Communion: Studies in Personhood and the Church* (Yonkers: St Vladimir's Seminary Press, 1985).

Index